DON ،

FRIENDS AND LOVERS

THE BATTLEFIELD

Carlo Goldoni

VOLUME TWO

DON JUAN

FRIENDS AND LOVERS

THE BATTLEFIELD

translated with an introduction by
Robert David MacDonald

OBERON BOOKS
LONDON

These translations first published in 1999 by Oberon Books Ltd.
(incorporating Absolute Classics)
521 Caledonian Road, London, N7 9RH
Tel: 0171 607 3637 / Fax: 0171 607 3629
e-mail: oberon.books@btinternet.com

British Library Cataloguing-in-Publication Data
A catalogue record for this book is available from the British Library.

ISBN 1 870259 37 8

Cover design: Andrzej Klimowski

Typography: Richard Doust

Printed in Great Britain by MPG Ltd., Bodmin.

Contents

INTRODUCTION

In making a second selection of plays by Goldoni, I have picked out three, written over a twenty-five-year period, which show Goldoni's more serious side, and which highlight his extraordinary versatility. If *Don Juan* is, in form at least, a fairly conventional, if manifestly stage-worthy *melodramma giocoso*, the two later plays are good examples of the naturalistic style which Goldoni developed in the late 1740s. This style could carry considerable weight on a seemingly fragile but unexpectedly tough framework, with grace under pressure, covering an area of expression limited only by the author's own horizons.

In his *Memoirs*, one of the most charming of eighteenth-century works of fiction, Goldoni tells us that, while working as resident dramatist for the Giuseppe Imer Company, he had for some time toyed with the idea of a Don Juan play, for which there were several ready-made models to hand. All he needed was the irritant that would compel him to scratch that particular patch among the slew of ideas, themes and possibilities that ran in his mind. In 1736 an unfortunate love affair gave it to him. The characters of Carino, Elisa and Don Juan correspond to Goldoni himself (the diminutive of his name, Carlino, is near enough), his lover Elisabetta Passalacqua, an actor with the Imer company, and Vitalba, the leading actor of the company. He assures us the scene of recrimination between Carino and Elisa is a verbatim account of what took place, and we are hardly surprised to hear that, whereas Vitalba was delighted with his role of Don Juan, Passalacqua threw a considerable scene, and had to be reminded of her contract before she would agree to play Elisa. Meanwhile Goldoni tells us the rest of the company happily appreciated the allusions in the play – hardly a matter for surprise – and that audiences unaware of them appreciated the play for itself.

It is the first treatment of the story to forgo the supernatural element of the statue coming to dinner, and though Juan is finally struck down by lightning, "because a wicked man ought to be punished... I [Goldoni] managed this event in such a way that it might be considered equally the immediate effect of God's anger, or the result of a combination of secondary causes." Also interesting is the way in which everyone who comes into contact with Juan is either destroyed or in some way diminished. He murders the Comendador, deprives Carino of his love, even the other two men, Alfonso and Octavio, end the play emptier than they began it: as for the women, Isabella, with, or rather, about whom Juan comes the nearest to actually admitting love, spends the play in male costume, a clear comment on her sexual insecurity, and, dissatisfied with the revenge she so ardently sought, accepts Octavio's final proposal with shrugging indifference; Elisa becomes coarser than ever as the result of Juan's desertion, and later of Carino's rejection of her; Anna seems to be turned to stone – after the wooing scene in Act Five, reminiscent of Richard III and Lady Anne, she sees clearly how dangerously close she had come to willing surrender, and in the final, deeply ironic scene of summing-up, she speaks not a word. Meanwhile Juan remains very much of a piece throughout, fluent, agile, his own man, tired of life and the world, unhindered by concepts of honour and morality. In the end, he tries – and fails – to make the others murder him, and endanger their souls, and is destroyed – by God or 'secondary causes'. A figure certainly in the Mozartian mould, and even in that of de Sade.

Friends and Lovers (Il Vero Amico) was one of the sixteen plays Goldoni wrote, at the exact middle of his oddly symmetrical life, for the 1750-51 season at the Teatro Sant'Angelo. Although somewhat sketchy, it contains a pair of mismatched couples which foreshadow his much fuller investigation of the same situation in his trilogy about summer holidays *La Villeggiatura.* It also contains a very good miser, that comic cliché of the period, whose fate Goldoni leaves uncertain at the end, though in the first production of this version, by the Citizens' Company of Glasgow, by whom all these versions were first presented, he definitely died. (Other divagations from the original included the setting of the play in Hamburg, where Florindo becomes more immediately understandable as a foreigner, and which lent a darker, more 'Northern Romantic' overtone to the proceedings, with echoes of the courtship of Robert and Clara Schumann, not to forget foreshadowings of plays like *A Month in the Country*. All this necessitated several changes of names of characters, the substitution of Stella as a sister, not, as in the first edition, an old aunt, and the concertina-ing of three rather ordinary parts for three servants into one very good part for Trivellino, a ruse which astute managers will see also saves two salaries).

The plot, turning on misplaced and misunderstood letters, is perfunctory enough, but the use of common language and simple facts and situations to lay bare the workings of invisible, internal wheels is brilliant, and the presentation of family life and ties, always Goldoni's forte, was seldom more deftly presented by him. On arriving in Paris in 1762, he discovered that Diderot was being accused of plagiarising the play for his *Le Fils Naturel* (1757), and was in consequence huffily trying to denigrate Goldoni as a hack concocter of farces; this must have seemed like the start of another feud such as he had come all that way to avoid, and doubtless might have been, had not Goldoni had the sense to corner Diderot at a party and exert a charm that resulted in mutual expressions of esteem between the two. The matter of plagiarism was, in any case, a looser concept in those pre-copyright days, and Goldoni himself had based his play on at least two earlier comedies (Flaminio Scala – *Amico Fedele* – and Luigi Riccoboni – *La Forza dell'Amicizia*). He also modified the present play for a second edition in 1764, *after* seeing Diderot's piece, and was rewarded, if that is the word, with two further imitations in the next fifty years or so (Alberto Nota – *Filosofo Celibatario* – and Paolo Ferrari – *Gli Amici Rivali*). Goldoni's play is certainly more flexible than Diderot's, and its moral thesis, or dilemma, whether friendship should triumph over love at whatever cost, more sensitively etched in. Goldoni's disciple, Gian Antona Traversi, said that Goldoni "wrote great comedies without presuming to introduce in them great ideas, whilst modern playwrights write little comedies and presume to put in great ideas." Well enough as a snap judgment, but sometimes the ideas are no less profound for being so lightly introduced.

The last play in this book, *The Battlefield* (La Guerra) was written in 1760, when Goldoni, at his peak, was working for the Teatro San Luca, managed by the distant and unsympathetic Vendramins, and was probably sparked off by a stay he made in Parma at the invitation of the Spanish Infante to write some comic opera libretti. Parma was then considered the most cultivated city in Italy, and boasted a French-speaking theatre that may have planted the first seed in Goldoni's mind about going to Paris. Another memory that may have surfaced was one of some twenty-seven years before, when, as a young man, he had witnessed from the city walls a battle between the Sards and the Austrians. "One could not have observed a battle from nearer to: the smoke often prevented one from distinguishing objects well; but it was a rare spectacle indeed, which few people can boast of having enjoyed." "Enjoyed" is not perhaps the most sympathetic word in the circumstances, though it was an age when people turned out to watch battles much as they did public executions: recall the civilians at Waterloo in "*Vanity Fair*", and Pierre Bezukhov going as an observer to Borodino. The next afternoon Goldoni sees with disgust the heaps of naked, looted corpses, and the scattered limbs and heads: he mentions with praise the action of the neighbouring Venetians in sending quantities of lime to prevent infecting the air.

There are foretastes of Schiller's *Wallenstein's Camp* here, and in Polidoro, the venal quartermaster, and Orsolina, the market woman, traces of Brecht's *Mother Courage* are fairly obvious, while throughout, Goldoni's distaste for militarism is bitterly apparent. As a Venetian, and a patriotic one at that, he could never see war as a practical means to human progress, nor could he see that it could be a fine thing to die for one's country. *Patria*, that magic word of the next century, is singularly absent from his works. Neither in this, nor in his other war-play *L'Amante Militare*, does any character glorify the profession of arms. The few brave and honourable men, like the hero, Faustino, and Don Egidio, commander of the besieged city, only serve to show up the darker colours of the surrounding countryside. Possibly Goldoni's near-criminal younger brother, mercenary in every sense of the word, may have contributed to his personal distaste for soldiery, but his picture of an officer's mess peopled by men utterly devoid of any nobility of spirit that might have excused their profession is a telling one, even if the conventional "mounted messenger" bringing news of deliverance at the end – another Brechtian echo from *The Threepenny Opera* here? – rather draws the teeth of what could have been a more complete denunciation of war than it eventually became.

In this version, which the Citizens' Company presented at the Teatro Goldoni in Venice at the 1980 Biennale, a fact that at least partially accounts for the liberal sprinkling of Italian salutations, insults and general fillers, there are certain modifications, principally in the extravagant stage directions, which can only have been there to show off some Vendramin machinery, though Goldoni specifically disclaimed this in his preface, and in the numbers of speaking NCOs and other ranks. In addition, the Count died at the end, an eventuality unsuited to an eighteenth-century comedy, and the epilogue was delivered not by the heroine, Florida, but by the cynical, crippled officer Cirillo.

At the time these versions were first performed, it is true to say that only *Il Vero Amico* had ever been performed outside Italy. Only that and *La Guerra* had been performed even inside Italy since their first performances. There are more than a hundred and fifty plays. Perhaps by the tercentenary of Goldoni's birth (2007) a few more shafts will have been sunk and a few more buckets of ore brought up from a vein as hard to exhaust as it is rewarding to mine.

RDM
Glasgow 1993

DON JUAN

Don Giovanni Tenorio, ossia Il Dissoluto

(1736)

for

Andrew Wilde

CHARACTERS

DON JUAN TENORIO,
a Neapolitan nobleman

DON ALFONSO,
prime minister to the King of Castile

COMENDADOR,
of Lojoa, a Castilian

DONNA ANNA,
his daughter

DONNA ISABELLA,
a Neapolitan, disguised in men's clothes

DON OCTAVIO,
the Duke, nephew to the King of Castile

ELISA,
a Castilian shepherdess

CARINO,
her lover, a Castilian shepherd

PAGE,
to the Comendador

SERVANTS

ROYAL GUARDS

The play is set in Castile and the surrounding countryside.

ACT ONE

DON ALFONSO's apartments.

DON ALFONSO:

    My child, if by that name the tender love
    that binds us will allow me to address you,
    your father is returning to Castile,
    loaded with yet more honours, well deserved;
    and in this happy time you are to marry.
    Our King, whose minister I am, respects
    and loves your father, and to you reserves
    equal affection and esteem. I know,
    being party to his plans, he longs to see
    the happiness of both the father and
    the daughter. But I sense a conflict in
    your double love for father and for husband.

DONNA ANNA:

    Señor, my great affection for my father
    completely fills my heart, which has not yet
    learned to love another man than he.

DON ALFONSO:

    It is time, though, that you knew the difference
    between a daughter's love, and that of a wife.
    They are two separate emotions, yet
    may both live in one breast. One duty feeds,
    the other passion fuels. Both are honourable,
    and both are worthy of a noble heart.

DONNA ANNA:

    I understand this other love you speak of,
    and, if I am not wilfully mistaken,
    it is the taste that binds two hearts together
    in close affection. For a handsome face,
    or noble qualities, I understand
    a woman may feel love: but nowhere is it
    taught that an unknown, even hateful, object
    can have the power to rouse such flames in her.

DON ALFONSO:

    That is the way of common souls. In them
    reason plays no part; but noble minds

respect what Heaven has marked out for them,
and always find those marriage-ties to be
desirable that may advance their fortune.

DONNA ANNA:

Advance my fortune?

DON ALFONSO:

To the highest rank –
the *very* highest rank.

DONNA ANNA:

(Oh happiness!
Can the King have fallen in love with me!)
Do not conceal my husband's name from me.

DON ALFONSO:

I must speak to your father first; if he
consents, I shall reveal it. Let it be
enough for now for you to know he is
of royal blood.

DONNA ANNA:

A king, in charity,
can raise my humble state, just as the sun
raises the vapour from the lowly earth
to give it strength and light. I am poor, both
in merit and in fortune, but two things
I have preserved: fidelity and honour.

DON ALFONSO:

I find you worthy of the highest state;
happy the man who can deserve your hand.

DONNA ANNA:

(I'll not deceive myself, power has its lure!)

PAGE: (*Entering.*)

Señor, the father of Donn'Anna has
arrived, and, prior to going to kneel before
His Majesty, has come to you.

DON ALFONSO:

Admit
the Comendador, and, Donna Anna, you
stay here with me: I wish to have my share
in your good fortune.

DONNA ANNA:

Will you tell my father
who is to be my husband?

DON ALFONSO:

He shall know
before he leaves... but how can you have learned
so suddenly to feel the love that you
knew nothing of just now?

DONNA ANNA:

My strong desire
to learn about a passion common to all...
(And shown me not by love, but by ambition!)
(*The COMENDADOR enters.*)

DON ALFONSO:

My friend, the light and cheer of those who love you!

COMENDADOR:

Sweet it is to come home to one's country,
sweetest of all to come home to one's friends!
(*He embraces DON ALFONSO.*)

DONNA ANNA:

Señor, your hand, so I may humbly kiss it.

COMENDADOR:

Let me embrace you, daughter. Oh, how happy
I am to see you once again! I am
your father, true, by nature, but affection
gives you another in this loyal friend.
(*To DON ALFONSO.*)
The pride of the Sicilian renegades...

DON ALFONSO:

I know, you have subdued: the instigators
of that presumptuous conspiracy
are coming to Castile to beg for pardon.
Now you have need of rest. The King desires
you think of nothing but of taking care
of yourself, to assure the safety of his crown.

COMENDADOR:

He shows me too much kindness; undeserved
by one who, in the service of his sovereign,

does no more than his duty.
The regard...
DON ALFONSO:
    ... he always held you in, is now increased;
as are your merits. He has planned to raise
a statue to you, and declare the precinct
where it will stand to be a sanctuary,
where persecuted souls and fugitives
may seek and find asylum, free from harm,
where even the justice of His Majesty
shall have no power to touch the refugee.
Money you have refused, in which respect
he did not show himself so liberal.
In point of fame and glory, you are raised
to be the pinnacle of knighthood, but you are,
at the same time, in point of worldly goods,
less fortunate.
COMENDADOR:
    What good are worldly goods?
The wisest man contents himself with little.
Of all the dangers that beset Mankind,
riches are the most fatal.
DON ALFONSO:
     While you were
alone, I could have praised such thinking in you:
but, since Heaven has given you a daughter,
it is your duty to think more of her
than of yourself. It is now time to give her
a suitable position, and a dowry
that corresponds with someone of your station.
COMENDADOR:
Her virtue is sufficient dowry for her;
if that is not enough to fit her with
a worthy husband, then she has no wish
to change her state to one where her good fortune
may be the envy of others.
DONNA ANNA:
    (Ah! He gives me
too much credit for too little virtue!)

DON ALFONSO:

Comendador, the King thinks of your daughter
more practically: he has picked her out
a husband worthy of her, and you. Her dowry
he will provide himself; he only asks,
through me, for your agreement as her father.

COMENDADOR:

The King is my most sovereign lord. He may
dispose of my will, as he may of my blood.
Such generosity I'll not refuse;
the gift is dear to me, because it is
to the advantage of my daughter, who
is just as dear to me as my own life.
Do you hear, Donna Anna? What do you think
of the royal bounty? Answer.

DONNA ANNA:

How could I
set up my will in flagrant opposition
against my sovereign's? Happy with my fate,
I happily go to meet the royal favour.

DON ALFONSO:

Stay here then. The bridegroom will be here
within the hour.

DONNA ANNA:

What?

COMENDADOR:

Who is he then?

DON ALFONSO:

The Duke Octavio.

DONNA ANNA:

But... of the royal blood...?

DON ALFONSO:

Your husband is to be the King's own nephew.
Do not be surprised at his high rank.
Your merits are quite equal to his birth.

DONNA ANNA:

(Oh, God! I have deceived myself! The Duke,
a man whom I have always held in horror!)

21

DON ALFONSO:

> I must return now to the King's apartments.
> (*To DONNA ANNA.*)
> Prepare to love your husband.

DONNA ANNA:

> (Oh, how all
> my hopes are dashed!)

DON ALFONSO:

> Do you turn pale? And fix
> your eyes upon the ground? Is the Duke's name
> somehow unwelcome to you?

COMENDADOR:

> No, that pallor,
> that timid drooping eye, is the true habit
> of the sex: they simulate their pleasure
> under the guise of modesty; this news,
> which might in others serve as an occasion
> of vanity and pride, has made her heart
> humble and reverent.

DON ALFONSO:

> Then stay with her:
> she may explain her reasons to her father
> without the need to blush. I trust she will
> realise the extent of her good fortune.
> (*DON ALFONSO leaves.*)

COMENDADOR:

> Daughter, raise your head, and heart, to Heaven,
> whence all good comes. A lucky star has kindled
> the desire in the King, by raising up
> the daughter, to reward the labours of
> the father. He has chosen you a husband,
> who could be heir to this kingdom, and
> who will be, if his uncle still continues
> to execrate the very name of marriage.

DONNA ANNA:

> I understand my destiny: none the less,
> I do not go to meet it happily.

COMENDADOR:

> But what is there in opposition to
> your happiness?

DONNA ANNA:

Ah, I know not how to tell you.

COMENDADOR:

Open your heart.

DONNA ANNA:

By habit and long usage
I have become almost a part of you.
I could not now be separated from you
without a bitter pain.

COMENDADOR:

Oh, my dear daughter!
Your love means everything to me. I too
would feel the separation tear away
a part of me. Only I force myself
to conquer grief, and humbly bow my head
to destiny.

DONNA ANNA:

We make our fates ourselves!
Heaven is not a tyrant, nor does it
intrude upon the free will of Mankind.

COMENDADOR:

Yet God disposes things in such a way
we are compelled to do His bidding blindly.

DONNA ANNA:

Does Heaven demand that I should sacrifice
my peace – myself – to a husband I detest?

COMENDADOR:

And yet just now you seemed to find the prospect
more than acceptable; did you not agree
to Don Alfonso?

DONNA ANNA:

Then – out of respect –
I was pretending; now I speak more freely,
and to my father. To extend my hand
to Duke Octavio, heartfelt disgust
will not allow it, nor do I intend it.
And should fate...

COMENDADOR:

No more. You are to be
the bride of Duke Octavio: you have sworn it.

I myself have sworn for you. If your heart
does not feel able to consent, your father
will force you to consent, unless you wish
to see his fond love changed to fierce disdain.
(*He goes, leaving DONNA ANNA alone.*)

DONNA ANNA:

Rashness, stupidity, how could I so soon
squander all my faith in vain illusion?
I understood from what Alfonso said,
the marriage bed he was proposing to me
could be no greater. Duke Octavio
the Heir Apparent? What assurance have I
the King's dislike of marriage may not change –
why may he not produce an heir? Or heirs?
But even given the Duke comes to the throne,
I still detest him, and shall always do so
even if the crown is on his head.
He cannot please me. Love and Hate are passions
that well from secret springs within our hearts.
My father can do what he will, the King
himself do all he can, but it shall never
be said I set my hand to this vile union.

ACT TWO

The countryside near Castile.

CARINO:
Farewell, Elisa.

ELISA:
Wait! Carino, ungrateful,
leaving me so soon?

CARINO:
Look at the sun,
striding with giant steps towards its setting.
If I stay any longer, night will fall,
and the fierce wolves will come out of the forest,
to wreak their cruel havoc on my flock.

ELISA:
You think more of your sheep than of Elisa,
and she would give up everything for you.
Even my pretty, pet deer, and all the things
a girl enjoys so much, I'd give them all
for the sweet pleasure I share here with you.

CARINO:
We shall see each other soon. When I have made
the sheepfold safe, and milked the mares, I shall
come back, Elisa.

ELISA:
Make your absence short,
my love, I have no peace away from you.
Then we can pass the best part of the night
in telling stories. Mother loves so much
to see us together.

CARINO:
Who is happier
than I? I do not envy richer farmers
their better fortunes. But Elisa, tell me,
will you always feel this affection for me?
Will you be true to me?

ELISA:
How can you doubt me?
Sooner than see me wanting faith to you,

you'll see the wolf lie down with the lamb; you'll see
sweet apples sprouting from the thorn bushes:
the rivers flowing upwards to the mountains.
Carino, only comfort of my heart,
I live and breathe for you; I wish to live
happy with you, or not to live at all.

CARINO:
Your sweet words fill my heart with joy! My idol,
let us be done with sighing; you will see
whether Carino's love is love sincere.
(*He goes out, leaving her alone.*)

ELISA:
High time a constant flame burned in my breast.
Until today, I loved as if in sport –
Silvio, Montano, Titiro, Ergasto,
Licisca, Megacle, Fileno – all
of them – who were my lovers, and whose passions
I made out I enjoyed, from vanity;
but now I feel the need to change my ways.
I cannot tell what marks Carino out,
which goes straight to my heart. His modest way
of speaking, his downcast eye, his honesty
and sincerity set him apart from all the rest,
and the first place in my heart I keep for him.
I love him and I want to add to his virtues
the credit for having made me true and faithful.

DON JUAN: (*Offstage.*)
Ah, villains!

ELISA:
          What is this? What are those cries?

DON JUAN: (*Off.*)
Oh, spare my life at least!

ELISA:
          A man! He's running
and crying out! What can have happened?

DON JUAN: (*Entering.*)
          Oh, misfortune!
Alone, and robbed of all my clothes and jewels,
which way am I to turn?

ELISA:

What accident,
Señor, what's happened to you? Can I help you?

DON JUAN:

A brutal troop of merciless assassins
has robbed me, as you see. At the first danger,
my servants all took flight; they stole my horse,
and all I had of value I have lost.

ELISA:

(Poor man! How I pity him!) I cannot
give you the help that you deserve – and need.
The shelter of my cottage, a coarse coat,
smoked meat, fresh water from the spring, a dinner
of herbs, is all I have to offer you.
If that's enough, then you are master of it.

DON JUAN:

My beauty, you can well alleviate
my ills... yes... nor do I refuse your offer,
and I shall be more grateful than you think.

ELISA:

It was not hope of gratitude or gain
that prompted me to make that meagre offer.
Pity aroused in me a natural instinct
to succour the oppressed, and, even in
distress, your face reveals a noble heart.
This is what urges me to offer you
what, in my poverty, I can.

DON JUAN:

(An act I think
will compensate me well for all I've lost.
Her beauty outweighs all the robbers took.)

ELISA:

Why don't you speak? Maybe you despise
my poor gifts?

DON JUAN:

No indeed. I value them
as I do life itself. And yet I hope for
a greater favour.

ELISA:
>   If it lies in my power.

DON JUAN:
>   Your heart.

ELISA:
>   What would you do with my poor heart?

DON JUAN:
>   Place it within my own.

ELISA:
>   A country heart
>   would not fit well inside a noble bosom.

DON JUAN:
>   The rich prize of your beauty makes amends
>   for all the buffetings of my ill-fortune.
>   At the first lightning flash of those fair eyes
>   I was struck motionless. My late attackers
>   cut me no deeper than you have my heart.

ELISA:
>   (Believe him if I dare!) This is just how
>   all of them talk who want to have their way
>   with simple country girls. Nerina, Elia,
>   both of them loved by gentlemen, and both
>   deceived by them; I should be on my guard.

DON JUAN:
>   (Yield she must though.) Men are not all the same.
>   And the near-fatal danger which I lately
>   encountered has deprived me of the power
>   of lying; your compassion no less than
>   your beauty urges me to say I love you.

ELISA:
>   (Fate, do not betray me now.) Señor,
>   if you feel love for me, then... (But Carino?
>   Have I forgot so soon?)

DON JUAN:
>   I swear to you
>   eternal faith.

ELISA:
>   Could you forgive yourself
>   if you broke faith to make a girl unhappy?

DON JUAN:
    To a man within whose veins there runs the blood
    of centuries, betrayal is unknown.
ELISA:
    Then you're a gentleman?
DON JUAN:
                            Such I was born
    and such I mean to die.
ELISA:
                            Where are you from?
DON JUAN:
    I am a Neapolitan.
ELISA:
                    And where
    are you travelling to?
DON JUAN:
                        Castile.
ELISA:
                                And why
    is that?
DON JUAN:
            To show my duty to your King.
ELISA:
    What is your name?
DON JUAN:
                        I shall not hide it from you;
    Don Juan Tenorio.
ELISA:
                    Don Juan!
DON JUAN:
                            You sigh?
    Why should that be?
ELISA:
                        Heaven alone can know
    whether you bring your whole heart here with you.
DON JUAN:
    Till now my heart was quite in my possession;
    no more though now, since you stole it from me.

ELISA:
> (I want to make my fortune; but Carino
> sticks in my heart.)

DON JUAN:
>   Be kind to me; and let
> me take you from these woods. Under my roof
> I will instruct you in the command of others:
> your rough wool shall be changed to cloth of gold,
> and decked with jewels, while in your power shall be
> all human pleasure.

ELISA:
>   If I weren't afraid
> of being deceived...

DON JUAN:
>   I do not know how I
> can further reassure you: here is my hand.

ELISA:
> Our custom here is to call Heaven to witness.

DON JUAN:
> I swear to the gods that rule both Heaven and earth
> you shall be my wife.

ELISA:
>   And if you fail?

DON JUAN:
> Let lightning strike the faithless soul from Heaven,
> and hurl it into the abyss.

ELISA:
>   (Carino,
> have pity on me in my cruel case.)
> Oh, yes, I do believe you: here's my hand.

DON JUAN:
> A gentle hand that touches me to the heart.
> (Love, you are bountiful, how much I owe you,
> if you can yield me up so fair a prey
> among the forests!)

ELISA:
>   What are you thinking now?

DON JUAN:
> I was reflecting on my happiness.

ELISA:
    If a faithful heart can make you happy,
    you have one. Mine.
DON JUAN:
                    The only thing I ask
    is your fidelity...

ELISA:
                    The first command
    of my new, noble husband.
DON JUAN:
                        Let us not
    delay then: you will be happy.
ELISA:
                        (Oh, Carino,
    comfort yourself that you are not the first;
    more than her lover, a woman loves her fortune.)
    (*She leaves with DON JUAN.*)
DONNA ISABELLA: (*In men's clothes, defending herself against
    various brigands.*)
    Help! Heaven!
DON OCTAVIO: (*Enters, beating them off.*)
                    Villains, many against one?
    Such violence, such vileness?
DONNA ISABELLA:
                        Friend, I owe
    all to your valour.
DON OCTAVIO:
                    Who were the treacherous villains
    who set upon you?
DONNA ISABELLA:
                    Highwaymen – who rob
    some of their money, others of their lives.
    They had already got my horse... where were
    the royal troops? How does the King allow
    such things to happen so near to the city?
DON OCTAVIO:
    The wretches change their ground continually:
    but he will find them.

DONNA ISABELLA:

                      Let me know at least
to whom I owe such opportune assistance.

DON OCTAVIO:

The Duke Octavio, nephew to the King.
And who are you, sir?

DONNA ISABELLA:

                      To my liberator
I am compelled to reveal my closest secrets.
These garments cover up a sex denied.
I am by birth a Neapolitan,
Donna Isabella, of the house
of Altomonte.

DON OCTAVIO:

                  But why deny your sex?
What strange adventure takes you from your country?
And why, at your age, do you travel alone?

DONNA ISABELLA:

The question causes me some pain, but still,
I must tell you everything, in the hope
I can employ you in my cause.

DON OCTAVIO:

                        My faith,
my counsel, my position and myself
are yours to call on to assist you in
the furtherance of your designs.

DONNA ISABELLA:

                        I was
betrayed, and the betrayer of my honour
has taken flight towards Castile. I wish
to find him once again.

DON OCTAVIO:

                  Who is the ingrate?

DONNA ISABELLA:

Don Juan Tenorio, the only son
of an illustrious family, and born
under the same cruel sky that saw my birth.
The villain was engaged to be my husband;
at the fair time of year that fills the fields
with flowers, our hands should have been joined together.

I loved him, oh!, too much, and thought my love
returned in equal measure: every moment
weighed like eternity upon my heart.
The lover chafed at the delay – how many times,
did the ingrate mock my love, and swear he burned
for me alone! How many times he took
his leave of me in tears! I told myself
that I was happy. Then, and through no fault
of mine, the traitor, forming new affections
that I learned of too late, deserted me,
carrying with him his promises and mine,
my grief, my hopes, my heart and my revenge.
Señor, if you can have compassion for
a loving heart betrayed, I beg you to
bear witness in my just cause to the King,
and should the traitor come within his power,
let him be brought to justice for his crime.

DON OCTAVIO:
I feel both sympathy and pity for you,
Donn'Isabella, in your bitter case.
Don Juan shall be your husband; or, I swear,
he will indemnify you with his death.

DONNA ISABELLA:
You lift the greater weight of my misfortune
from my heart.

DON OCTAVIO:
                    (So fair a face does not deserve
a faithless lover.) You may take my horse.
My squire will have another. Let us go,
the capital is no distance.

DONNA ISABELLA:
                    Heaven reward you.
In succouring the oppressed, men show like gods.
(*Exeunt.*)

CARINO: (*Re-enters alone.*)
Thanks be to Heaven, they're gone. I would not wish
ever to meet such folk. Townspeople? Take care!
They're so blown up with pride and arrogance,
they think us in the country are all savages.
We sweat and slave to earn their bread for them,

they grow rich on the work we do – and treat us
worse than ever they would their dogs or horses.
They think we've got no morals in the country.
Of course, they are all models of discretion.
The peasant steals, they say; and not the townsman?
Yes, and a good deal worse!... But where is she?
My sun and moon!... not by the spring?... Elisa!
Where are you hiding? You will have been avoiding
the unwelcome sight of all those folk from town.
Aha! you're cunning! You're behind that tree.
Got you! I thought it was her. Has she gone
to pick fruit further up the hill? I'll go and...
No, here she comes. Elisa, hurry!... What?
A shepherd with her? No, that's not a shepherd.
He's dressed like one, but that false, curly hair,
that pale face and that stately walk of his
are sure signs of the city. What's this mean?
Can she have betrayed her faith so soon?
I shall hide here, to see and not be seen.

DON JUAN: (*In country clothes.*)

Nymph, I can only thank you for your love.

ELISA:

Why do you not call me wife?

CARINO:

(Oh, God!
what do I hear?)

DON JUAN:

Because you are not that yet.

ELISA:

What more is there to do to tie the knot?

DON JUAN:

Nothing but what is fitting to my rank.
Traditional ceremonies, rituals,
the usual pomp of marriage.

ELISA:

Let us go, then,
and get it over with.

CARINO:

(The villain!)

DON JUAN:

Yes,

    but it is not quite fitting you should come
    with me just now. Let me arrange things first.
    My angel, in no time at all I shall
    expect you in the city.

ELISA:

Might you be

    designing to deceive me?

DON JUAN:

Needless fears!

    I could not be disloyal, if I tried.

ELISA:

    If you are thinking to betray me, then
    the gods will punish you.

CARINO:

(And you, too, traitress

    that you now are!)

DON JUAN:

(Only in bed shall I

    not have to bear the tedious clamour of
    her dull complaints.) Dear heart, I leave this heart
    of mine with you, but take away with me
    the pledge both of your love, and of my loyalty.
    Farewell, Elisa.

ELISA:

And can I hope, my love,

    for you to love me always?

DON JUAN:

Once again

    I'll swear if you desire it.

ELISA:

Go in happiness

    and I will follow you.

DON JUAN:

But not so soon

    that others notice it. (You hope in vain
    ever to see me again.) Dear heart, farewell!
    (*Exit.*)

CARINO:

(Eyes, what was it you saw? What must I do?)

ELISA:

(And if he *does* deceive me? Then this heart
will be Carino's once again. I must
at all events, make sure of at least one lover.)

CARINO:

(The black unfaithfulness! I'll have to take
the wretched girl to task; I shall abandon her.)

ELISA:

(He is a gentleman; he would not lie.)

CARINO:

Are you back so late?

ELISA:

Listen, Carino.
My pet, white deer I love so much, I heard it –
crying: I ran to it in fear... Quite often
I wondered whether I would arrive in time.

CARINO:

Be honest: may it not have been a stag,
that by its barking tempted you away?

ELISA:

We don't get stags here.

CARINO:

Only I thought I saw
you with an animal which was no deer.

ELISA:

You are mistaken.

CARINO:

No, there was no mistake;
it was an animal like us.

ELISA:

You mean
a man?

CARINO:

I do.

ELISA:

Oh, him! that was a cousin
of Corydon's, the one goes with Nerina;

he's just a stupid shepherd, but the others
find him amusing with the things he says.
CARINO:
I see: and you find him still more amusing.
ELISA:
He certainly makes me laugh.
CARINO:
                              One day – who knows? –
he may also make you cry?
ELISA:
                              Why ever should he?
CARINO:
Enough... what is his name?
ELISA:
                              What are you asking?
You mean you didn't recognise Pagoro?
CARINO:
I never saw him look so spruce, so proud!
ELISA:
(I fear things are beginning to come out.)
CARINO:
What did he promise, and swear to do for you?
ELISA:
To find a companion for my little deer.
CARINO:
(The little deer has certainly found that.)
It seemed I heard the name of wife.
ELISA:
                              Well, that
would make my deer a wife.
CARINO:
                              From what I heard
it seemed the wife was going to be you.
ELISA:
The stupid fellow said, if all the beauties
in the world proposed themselves to him in marriage,
he wouldn't be the leastest bit surprised.
CARINO:
Has he gone on to the city?

ELISA: Yes, to sell
   Nerina's flowers for her.
CARINO:
                         And taken with him
   Elisa's heart.
ELISA:
              What was that?
CARINO:
                      Oh, be quiet!
   I know it all, I heard it all. You liar,
   you cannot hide things from me now.
ELISA:
                         Carino!
   How can you talk to me that way?
CARINO:
                       That is
   the way Carino talks to perjurers,
   who have betrayed him. Do you not remember
   the faith you swore to me? Ungrateful! Cruel!
   Could you not keep faith a single day?
ELISA:
   Listen to me... you must not think...
CARINO:
                     Be quiet!
   I do not want to hear another word.
   You want to weave another web of lies
   and flattery around my heart. If ever
   I lend an ear again to such deceptions,
   then I deserve to be betrayed, and worse.
ELISA:
   (I cannot hide my fault a second longer.)
   Carino, oh, my life! It is all too true:
   the man you saw me with wished to deceive me.
   I had been drawn to him at first by pity:
   attacked by robbers, he'd called out for help,
   and to reward me for the aid I gave him
   he offered me his hand and, flattering me
   with all the crafty townsman's thousand arts

and wiles, brought me to feel some silly sort
of infatuation for him. But, Carino,
I still remembered you, and kept my heart
constant and faithful.

CARINO:

I am miserable!
If only I had never heard your words.
I leave you; I abandon you; I curse
the day I met you.

ELISA:

No, you must not leave me!
I am so wretched! do you not remember
those days we spent together...

CARINO:

Yes, I do,
and to my greater pain. Much as I loved you,
I swear I hate you now.

ELISA:

Look, at your feet
your poor Elisa asks forgiveness for
her innocent mistake. Have pity, dearest.

CARINO:

Do not hope for it – ever.

ELISA:

If you are
my life, ah, then I cannot live without you.

CARINO:

Your life is of no interest to me.

ELISA:

In that case, I must die here at your feet.

CARINO:

And I shall watch you do so with great pleasure.

ELISA:

(I knew how he would hate me.) With this blade –
look at me! – I'll kill myself!

CARINO: (*Not looking.*)

Go on, then.
Pierce your unworthy heart, and wash away
the stain you have put upon my love and faith.

ELISA:

> I am not afraid of dying. The only thing
> that *can* make me afraid is your contempt;
> oh, do not let me die without a glance.
> Look at me once more in charity,
> then I shall kill myself.

CARINO:

>   You need not hope
> for that from me.

ELISA:

>   Oh, God! You are inhuman!
> Would you deny me even that small comfort?
> Do my tears not move you to an ounce of pity?
> It is so little, the favour that I ask;
> look at me once, and then I shall be gone.

CARINO:

> (She is melting me.) You miserable creature,
> there, I shall look at you. What is it you want?
> (The sight is fatal.) You do not move my pity.
> (I cannot resist it.)

ELISA:

>   (He is beginning to yield.)
> Oh, God, I can control myself no longer:
> the terrible bitter pain has done the office
> better than any sword: I fall, I die.
> (*She pretends to faint.*)

CARINO:

> Elisa! Heavens! What is this? Are you dead?
> No, she's not dead. Run to the nearby spring,
> fetch water and run back; cases of fainting
> can be brought round with water in the face.
> (*He goes out.*)

ELISA:

> The ninny has surrendered! Oh, the joy
> of knowing how to pretend at the right time.
> That is the happiest weapon of our sex.
> Here he is, coming back; go on pretending.
> (*She resumes her former position.*)

CARINO: (*Returning with a jug of water.*)
    Oh, God in Heaven succour her. If she dies...
    (*Bathing her face.*)
    what will I do then, unhappy man?
    Her lips moved. She is coming to – I think.
    My idol, see, your shepherd loves and aids you.
ELISA:
    Savage, you wished me dead, and now you stop me
    when I want to die?
CARINO:
                        I never wished you dead.

ELISA:
    But if you think me faithless and inconstant,
    I must despise my life.
CARINO:
                    Dear love, I think you
    faithful and constant.
ELISA:
                    Are you laughing at me?
    You are so cruel.
CARINO:
               No, I repent my cruelty.

ELISA:
    And you won't speak again of your suspicions?
CARINO:
    No, my treasure.
ELISA:
                 Will you be faithful to me?
CARINO:
    To death, my angel. But let us not lose
    precious time to no purpose. Let us go,
    let love unite our hands: your mother will
    agree...
ELISA:
         Yes. Let us go, the only thing
    I want is just to follow you.
CARINO:
                    Thanks, Heaven!
    I have regained the peace I'd lost, I am
    the happiest of lovers.

(*He goes out.*)
ELISA:

Poor Carino!
But that is just how crafty women like them!
(*She follows him.*)

ACT THREE

Courtyard in the residence of DON ALFONSO.

DON ALFONSO:

    Your husband has arrived here in Castile,

    and is to wait upon you soon; be happy.

DONNA ANNA:

    Señor, at times the beating of our hearts

    forewarns us of misfortune. Happiness

    is not a thing I feel at mention of

    the Duke's name; even to hear it causes me

    pain of a kind unknown to me before.

DON ALFONSO:

    Come, when you see him, you will change your mind.

    The language of the heart's not always clear;

    sometimes it seems to presage misadventure,

    and yet, despite those heartbeats that we fear

    and misinterpret, all is for the best.

DONNA ANNA:

    Let him rather visit us as duke,

    than oblige me to welcome him as husband.

DON ALFONSO:

    Here he is now; do not be discourteous.

    Give us at least a proof of your obedience,

    true to your friend, your father and your King.

DON OCTAVIO: (*Entering with DONNA ISABELLA in men's clothes.*)

    Señor, an order from His Majesty

    brings me to you.

DON ALFONSO:

               That is the royal will.

    Here is Donn'Anna, whom the King has chosen

    to be your wife.

DON OCTAVIO:

             (Alas, what do I hear?

    Marry a woman for whom I feel aversion

    rather than love?)

DONNA ANNA:

             (He does not seem too happy.)

DON ALFONSO:

    Come closer, Duke, and let your lovely bride
    hear from your own lips the assurance of
    your love.

DON OCTAVIO:

          The King, my master, Donna Anna,
    has disposed of me; and I respect his order.
    I offer you my hand.

DONNA ANNA:

                Señor, a contract
    prescribed by royal authority is not
    one that I may refuse.

DON ALFONSO:

              Señor, I had hoped
    to hear more amorous words to a young woman.

DON OCTAVIO:

    My tongue is not accustomed to expressions
    of tenderness: I do not have the art.

DONNA ANNA:

    Señor, let me excuse you any such
    compulsion, since it costs you such an effort.

DON ALFONSO:

    Duke, who is the gentleman with you?

DON OCTAVIO:

    Señor... but first, he has a secret, I
    must inform you, which obliges one to silence.
    He wishes to speak to you in confidence,
    and in my presence.

DONNA ANNA:

              Señor, duty demands
    that I withdraw, which, by your leave, I do.

DON ALFONSO:

    Do so, I shall be with you in a moment.

DONNA ANNA:

    (That, to me, looks like a woman, and
    a pardonable curiosity
    suggests I would do well to listen to them.)
    (*She withdraws to listen unseen.*)

DON OCTAVIO:

    Let me present to you, Señor, a lady,

    albeit in men's attire, of noble birth.

    Her honour has been outraged by a gentleman.

    She seeks him in Castile; if he is found here,

    she demands justice on the vile offender.

DONNA ISABELLA:

    Señor, Donn' Isabella, only child

    of the duchy of Altomonte, bows before you,

    and begs your favour in assisting her.

DON ALFONSO:

    I shall do all I can: who is the traitor

    who has insulted and abandoned you?

DONNA ISABELLA:

    Don Juan Tenorio.

DON ALFONSO:

                 I know the name.

    Fame speaks well of his family.

DONNA ISABELLA:

                     I speak

    of nothing but his sad deception of me,

    his cowardly flight, and of my love betrayed.

DON OCTAVIO:

    The lady's suffering deserves compassion.

DON ALFONSO:

    If Don Juan comes here, then I shall entreat

    justice of the King.

DONNA ANNA: (*Coming forward.*)

                No, Don Alfonso!

    Do not give credence to the lies of others.

    This woman's a secret mistress of the Duke!

    He hardly could do better than devise

    this vague and highly opportune deception,

    to have her near, and not provoke his uncle.

    His heart forearmed, he scarcely looked at me

    just now; and when he offered me his hand,

    the offer seemed both late and forced from him.

    Heaven, in Time, brings all our plots to light.

    The Duke's unwilling to go back upon

a contract he detests; but let him love
wherever he has a mind: I yield him to her.

DON ALFONSO:

You are too hasty, Donna Anna; you
let yourself be swayed by vain suspicion.
You would be better advised to do as you
were told.

DON OCTAVIO:

       (Her anger is no proof of love.)

DONNA ISABELLA:

Friend, you suspect me wrongfully. I never
saw your Duke before today. It was
pity moved him to render me assistance,
not love; I swear to Heaven.

DONNA ANNA:

                  Oh, yes, I must
believe it of his partner in deception.
Do not make excuses for your lover;
nor try to ease my breast of my suspicion.
What better proof could I have ever wished for
of his indifference, his hatred, that
abhors my face and execrates my heart?
Rather than have to look at him, I shall leave.
Heaven be thanked, I have found out the truth.
(And Heaven be thanked as well, for giving me
this timely pretext for my own aversion.)
(*She leaves.*)

DON ALFONSO:

Duke, Donna Anna is enraged. It is
for you to undeceive her, calm her down.

DON OCTAVIO:

But how? I never saw a woman more
irrational and less inclined to prudence.

DON ALFONSO:

Jealousy walks hand in hand with love.

DON OCTAVIO:

With love at that degree of tenderness
I am not best pleased. I beg you, as you love me,
do not force me to honour such a contract.

DON ALFONSO:

A contract drawn up by His Majesty?
It cannot be annulled. She is your wife;
your promise has been given to her father.

DON OCTAVIO:

But if the heart does not consent...

DON ALFONSO:

The heart
will act from duty, not from vain desire.
(*He leaves.*)

DONNA ISABELLA:

Duke, how I sorrow at your grief! I am
the cause of all your difficulties, and
the innocent reason for your present anger.

DON OCTAVIO:

Donn'Isabella, more than my own troubles,
I am concerned for yours. I wish for nothing
more than to find the man who has outraged you.
I shall challenge him, and if he falls, perhaps
there may still be a husband left for you.
(*He leaves.*)

DONNA ISABELLA:

Pray Heaven I can remodel my affections
and leave my honour without stain or shame!
Perhaps the Duke will be the worthy flame
to light my tender heart. Stars, what do I see!
Him! My betrayer! I see him again.
The Gods have set him up before my eyes.
My heart is trembling. What to do I know not.
I shall take counsel from my love and anger.
(*She withdraws.*)

DON JUAN:

Whichever way I turn my curious gaze,
I see the splendid majesty of Spain.
My eyes, however, have not seen, as yet,
a beauty rare enough to enchain my heart.
To one who does not practise constancy,
the chains of love are no more than a game.
Love is no more than voluntary surrender

to natural desires, and beauty has
no other value than the wish to possess it.
The day I first saw Donna Isabella,
she went some way towards seducing me
to fall in love with her, against my custom;
but when she blindly gave herself to me,
the only thing I loved then was my freedom.
So with the shepherdess and all the rest
I have deceived and flattered... What the devil
do I see there? Either I am mistaken,
or Donna Isabella, in male attire,
dogs me to vex me further. It is she.
I shall avoid the encounter.
(*He makes to go.*)

DONNA ISABELLA: (*Coming forward.*)
                        Caballero,
slacken your pace; I have to speak with you.

DON JUAN:
I do not know you, sir, another time...

DONNA ISABELLA:
Don Juan! Have you effaced my image from
your memory, as well as from your heart?
Can you not see in me the unhappy woman,
deluded and deceived by you, who has
disguised herself to follow you? You monster!
How can you pretend you do not know me?

DON JUAN:
You say you are a woman? Dressed as a man?
And that I am the man who has betrayed you,
who promised to be true to you, and failed?
I do not recall.

DONNA ISABELLA:
                   Not recall Isabella?
The grief that frets my pride, the tears, the sighs,
the vigils, and the hardships of my journey,
perhaps all these have altered my appearance;
my name alone, though, should beget remorse
and shame in you: shake off your lethargy,
recall the oaths you made to Heaven, to God.

DON JUAN:
I have no recollection of such oaths.
DONNA ISABELLA:
Did you not swear fidelity to me,
did you not swear love?
DON JUAN:
                    I only know
I have never sworn to keep faith with a woman.
DONNA ISABELLA:
I understand. You wish to say, you liar,
you infidel, that if you called me wife,
you said it with your lips and not your heart;
that you pretended love to me, and now
my trust, too great, has lost me my rash love;
now you deride me, and despise my grief.
My faith dishonoured, that is not a dream.
My love despised, no, nor is that a dream.
Betrayer, it is useless to pretend
not to recall my face, my name, our love.
Traitor, to hide is useless; for I know you
all too well; if you refuse to give me
justice for the love you have betrayed,
I shall exact revenge on you in blood.
Draw your sword! Now let me lose my life
along with yours, or recompense my injuries!
DON JUAN:
Friend, I am not accustomed to pay heed
to lunatics. To draw my sword against you
would be the basest cowardice.
DONNA ISABELLA:
                      Whether or not
I am a lunatic, the trial of arms will tell.
You had the courage to abandon me;
would you be less bold now in killing me?
What am I saying? You are the one to die.
DON JUAN:
(It is high time this irritating, hateful
disturber of my peace had her quietus.)
Señor, *en garde*! You do but hurry on
the hour of your death.

DONNA ISABELLA:

Heaven fight for me!

(*They fight. The COMENDADOR enters.*)

COMENDADOR:

Gentlemen, put up your swords... Great Heavens,
Don Juan, here? Friend, when did you arrive
here in Castile? And what on earth's your quarrel?

DON JUAN:

Comendador, wise, brave, a nation's hero,
allow me humbly to salute this generous,
unvanquished hand.

COMENDADOR:

By no means.

DONNA ISABELLA:

(What is this
vexatious interruption?)

COMENDADOR:

But have you
so little regard for me? Is it by chance
that I must learn of your arrival? Is
my home so humble it does not deserve
to welcome you as guest?

DON JUAN:

Barely an hour
has passed since I set foot within the city.

COMENDADOR:

Barely an hour, and duelling already?

DONNA ISABELLA:

Comendador, despite the great esteem
in which I hold you, I must beg of you
not to impede the progress of this combat.

COMENDADOR:

At least acquaint me with the reasons for
your disagreement.

DONNA ISABELLA:

What I am not allowed
to say, there is no need for you to know.
Don Juan has insulted me; in consequence
I have demanded satisfaction.

DON JUAN:

This man is quite unknown to me. He has
demanded satisfaction, though for what
I do not know. He calls himself a man,
at times, however, he shows every sign
of being a woman. I have made no sort
of promise to him, yet he calls me word-breaker.

DONNA ISABELLA:

And so you are...

DON JUAN:

          I will not suffer this.

COMENDADOR:

One moment, let me beg of you. If it
is true that Don Juan has offended you,
then I myself will see that you have justice.
Since I am not accustomed to betray
reason and duty for the sake of friendship,
tell me wherein he failed.

DONNA ISABELLA:

          The offence is such
that my good name demands that I conceal it.

COMENDADOR:

My knowledge of it will not make it public.

DONNA ISABELLA:

But I do not consent that you should know it.

COMENDADOR:

You do not trust me, then?

DON JUAN:

          He can produce
no reason for his anger. Fury took him
beyond all bounds.

COMENDADOR: (*To DON JUAN.*)

          You cannot mean to fight
with somebody who cannot recognise
reason or duty. Are you going to listen
to a lunatic? Think of your reputation!
If you are beaten, there is the disgrace:
and if you win, they will say, to your face,
there's little credit winning from a fool.

DONNA ISABELLA:

I am no fool – I mean to have revenge.

COMENDADOR:

Then I command you, in my sovereign's name,
break off this combat. Let me intimate
the King's displeasure, should you fail to obey.

DONNA ISABELLA:

At such an order, given in such a name,
I sheathe my weapon, and suspend my anger.
The time will come, though, when the unworthy traitor
will pay me back in blood for all my injuries.
(*She leaves.*)

COMENDADOR:

Yes, yes, the time will come. But let us wait
no longer to present you to the King.
Come; he will appreciate, I trust,
my presentation of your loyal service.

DON JUAN:

Your kindness can have none but good effects.

COMENDADOR:

I well recall what your illustrious father
once did for me. What Italy has lost
in him! The Moors remember him as well,
and what his sword achieved... Here now to meet us
is Don Alfonso, the King's minister
and friend.

DON JUAN:

        I know of him by reputation;
a man who has made himself both loved and feared.

DON ALFONSO: (*Entering with DON OCTAVIO, DONNA ANNA and BODYGUARDS.*)

Comendador, the King excuses you
your attendance at the *levée*, for today.

COMENDADOR:

Yet one more instance of his favour to me.
Dear friend, allow me to present to you
one who deserves both your love and the King's:
Don Juan Tenorio, a Neapolitan...

DON ALFONSO:
>His father's name and fame I well remember.
>(*To DON OCTAVIO.*)
>(The man whom Donna Isabella named
>as her betrayer.)

DON OCTAVIO:
>   (Yes. Undoubtedly.)

DON JUAN:
>I kiss your hand, Señor, both in esteem
>and eagerness to do you service.

DON ALFONSO:
>Make use of me, Señor, and do not think of
>abandoning our capital too soon.
>(This matter must be cleared up.) Comendador,
>will you conduct your daughter to your house?
>She wishes to go home. Your friend will follow
>in a few moments.

DON JUAN:
>   I shall join you soon.

COMENDADOR:
>Señor, I hope you will not disappoint me.
>Our table may be poor, but not our welcome.
>(*He leaves.*)

DON ALFONSO: (*To DON OCTAVIO.*)
>(Withdraw, Duke.)

DON OCTAVIO:
>   (Yes. Meanwhile I'll go to look
>for Donna Isabella once again.)
>(*He leaves.*)

DON ALFONSO:
>Don Juan, you are the illustrious descendant
>of a distinguished and heroic line.
>It is unthinkable that you should wish
>to fall behind your ancestors in virtue;
>we cannot therefore hope for anything
>from you but actions fully worthy of them.
>One power alone, the violence of love,
>which conquers heroes and subdues the wise,
>could ever infect you with that deadly poison

which can deprive the clearest mind of sense.
Nor, in my view, is such a misadventure
crime or dishonour. The sensibility
of Nature, frail, unsound: the flower of youth,
the wiles and flatteries of woman's image:
these have such force that, if the heart does not
take flight at once, it scarcely can resist.
No need for you to summon up a blush
of irritation; I can sympathise
with the follies of a lover. All I ask
is sincere proof of your fidelity:
tell me, is it true that you have been
wanting in faith towards a noble lady?

DON JUAN:

Alas, I too have had my share in that
common misfortune, the pursuit of Love.
I loved, I love still; but my love does not
make me guilty, on the contrary,
the love the flame of honour lights is chaste.
I love the woman Heaven destined for me;
marriage to her was all that could give pleasure
to my family, my country, and my heart.

DON ALFONSO:

May one know her name?

DON JUAN:

                        Donn'Isabella
of the Duchy of Altomonte.

DON ALFONSO:

                         Was the marriage
ever concluded?

DON JUAN:

                     Would to God it had been!
I should not now be so far from my idol.

DON ALFONSO:

But why did you abandon her?

DON JUAN:

                        Cruel fate
tore us apart. A royal minister
insulted me. I challenged him. We met.

Fate used my hand to lay him on the ground.
His death displeased the King; and to escape
the first effects of royal resentment, I
fled from my country, parted from my love.
(No lie can be maintained without the aid
of another hundred.)
DON ALFONSO:

                 Donna Isabella,
weeping, demanding vengeance for the love
she says you have betrayed, has followed you.
DON JUAN:

Then either Donna Isabella's mad,
or else this woman is a phantom.
DON ALFONSO:

I have spoken to her myself.
DON JUAN:

                  And what assurance
have you she is the one whose name and rank
she claims? What reason have you to believe her?
DON ALFONSO:

She told her story with great clarity.
DON JUAN:

A woman's lips are fragile testimony.
DON OCTAVIO: (*Entering.*)

Señor, Donna Isabella is nearby,
wishing to speak to you.
DON JUAN:

              How opportune!
DON OCTAVIO:

(Don Juan appears confused.)
(*He goes to bring in DONNA ISABELLA.*)
DON JUAN:

             (Now is the time
for fluent speaking and determined action!)
DONNA ISABELLA:

(There is my betrayer!)
DON JUAN:

           Where is she
who usurps the name of Donna Isabella?

DON ALFONSO:
You see her there before you.

DONNA ISABELLA:
                              Yes, I am she.

DON JUAN:
Señor, forgive me, but that person there –
whether man or woman I do not know –
is under some illusion, dreaming, lying,
in matter of name and, possibly, of sex.
An altogether different style of beauty,
of face, of eyes, of noble, proud deportment
signalises Donna Isabella.
Her nobility is such that it could never
be overcome by the deceits of others.
What? Donna Isabella, in mens' clothes,
alone, leaving her country, going in trace
of a fugitive? No noble girl, of her age,
burning with honest love, would dare so much.
Ah, if your looks did not defend this liar,
I would lay him on the ground with my own hand.

DONNA ISABELLA:
Savage! Liar! Señor, these speeches are
a barbarous nature's calculated lies.
The traitor doubles the insults, blow upon blow,
and to his first disdain now adds a second.
I am not lying! I am Isabella.
This is my affianced husband who
abandoned me, forsworn.

DON JUAN:
                              Impertinent!
Easily said, but not so easily proved.
What testimony can you adduce that gives
a shred of credibility to your words?

DONNA ISABELLA:
All the Gods in Heaven.

DON JUAN:
                              Villains show
scant hesitation to profane the name
of God.

DONNA ISABELLA:
>God is not mocked. He will have vengeance
for your offences against both Him, and me.
(*To DON ALFONSO.*)
I demand justice for my love betrayed.

DON ALFONSO:
To obtain justice it is not enough
to rely solely on ill-founded quarrels.
Proof incontrovertible is needed –
clear proof, as clear as the sun at noon.

DON JUAN:
Just sentence of an even juster heart!

DONNA ISABELLA:
Ah, I see all too well! I, of all women,
am the most utterly abandoned, and
Heaven itself is now become my enemy.
Señor, in pity...

DON ALFONSO:
>What do you want from me?
Two parties both deny things to my face,
and neither with a scrap of proof between them,
to which of them should I give greater credence?
Whoever you are, if you have any claim
on this man's heart, then take the matter to
your King, who will compel a settlement.

DONNA ISABELLA:
God! Must I tolerate insult without vengeance?
Duke, your good offices...

DON OCTAVIO:
>In such a case,
I could not be of much assistance to you.

DONNA ISABELLA:
If my life is of no value to me,
other than to serve the man who is
the cause of all my sorrow, then that too
shall be a sacrifice to tyranny.
Yes, I shall die. If there is nobody
on earth to punish you, let Heaven do so.
Your crime and your disgrace assure me of it.
(*Exit.*)

DON JUAN:

Now do you doubt he is insane?

DON ALFONSO:

Doubt? No.

Follow him, Duke, see the unhappy creature
comes to no harm.

DON OCTAVIO:

I shall.

(*He goes out.*)

DON JUAN:

Though death would be
the least of all his possible misfortunes.
To live, and not to be aware of it,
is a fate far worse than death.

DON ALFONSO:

Yes, but we have
a duty to preserve life, even that
of the insane. Don Juan, I hope, for your sake,
the one who calls you traitor really *is* mad.

(*He goes out.*)

DON JUAN: (*Alone.*)

Her grief will drive her mad, just as she was
driven mad for a time by the god with the arrows.
If only I had the same amount of courage
to keep plots going that I have to start them!
I do not trust myself to win for ever.
Another such encounter could well be
fatal for me. Time I was moving on.
I cannot let that woman dog my steps
indefinitely.

ELISA: (*Entering.*)

Ah! My love, my husband,
I have found you at long last!

DON JUAN:

Elisa! Dearest!

(Another trial: subtlety, stand by me!)

ELISA:

Since you left my side, how many tears
of grief have I not shed! But Heaven has heard

my prayers. Hardly arrived here, here I find you,
and here I hope to find in you again
that love, that faith I found in you before.

DON JUAN:

My dearest, you are not deceived. I am
true to your love. (She's mad if she believes that.)

ELISA:

But if you love me, dearest, why the delay
in bringing on our marriage?

DON JUAN:

There are reasons
of honour which compel me to postpone it.

ELISA:

All reasons which true love can overcome.
Relieve my loving heart of its suspicions.
Do you like my face? Do my eyes shine for you?
I'm offering you my heart: if you delay
in accepting it, then maybe Heaven will
dispose of me elsewhere.

DON JUAN:

I should die of grief:
but if a better fortune comes your way,
your heart is still your own.

ELISA:

(Alas! A lawyer's answer!) Still my own?
What liberty of choice remains to me,
since I belonged to you? Love joined our hearts:
now it remains for love to tie our hands.

CARINO: (*Entering.*)

(Oh, God, Elisa – and her lover! Traitress!)

DON JUAN:

However, for the moment it is not
possible.

ELISA:

Everything is possible
for somebody whose heart beats with true love.
Cruel man, if you loved me as I do you,
you would seek ways to have me always by you.

CARINO:

Caballero...

ELISA:

        (Oh, Heavens!)

DON JUAN:

              What do you want?

CARINO:

  Do not trust her false and lying tongue.
  It is her habit to betray her lovers.

DON JUAN:

  And how do *you* know that?

ELISA:

             Make him be quiet.

DON JUAN:

  No, speak.

CARINO:

       I have proof of her lies: she left me,
  after she had sworn fidelity.

DON JUAN:

  Elisa, do you hear?

ELISA:

         I don't deny it:
  I only did it though to please my mother.
  You are the only one I really love.

DON JUAN:

  It is not honourable for me to break
  the bonds others have forged. I give you back
  your bride; if she has been unfaithful to you,
  forgive the habits of the sex in her;
  believe me, ladies of our rank can be
  just as inconstant.

ELISA:

        Is this how...

DON JUAN:

             What's this?
  Do you wish to change your husbands with your mood?
  A most delightful custom that would be!
  How many, oh, how many imitators
  would follow you, if that were possible!
  Come, be contented with the man who has
  been found for you by Heaven – and your mother.

ELISA:

It's cruel, laughing at me.

CARINO:

No, no, I yield
all my rights. And let a bond be broken
which I hate more than I hate death itself.
She's yours, I shan't oppose you; may the faith
she swore to me not turn out sour for you.

DON JUAN:

I would not be a gentleman, if I
could not control my own desires. I give her
back to you; so take her, if it makes you
happy. And remember – it is prudent
to hide what it is useless to reveal.

(*He leaves.*)

ELISA:

Carino! Oh, God!

CARINO:

Yes, yes, call for Carino.
If I saw you fall dead, I'd not believe you.

ELISA:

Are you too leaving me?

CARINO:

At least I have
the comfort of revenge for what I've suffered.

ELISA:

It's blasphemy, insulting the oppressed.

CARINO:

And what is the betrayal of faith? A virtue?

ELISA:

Despair will kill me.

CARINO:

You're still just pretending:
can you not be true in anything?

ELISA:

And could you have the heart to watch me die?

CARINO:

And lend a hand, if yours were not enough.

ELISA:

How quickly all your sympathy has changed
to cruelty.

CARINO:

At the same speed with which
you yourself changed one lover for another.

ELISA:

But what am I to do?

CARINO:

Do what you will.
Do everything that a despairing heart
can prompt someone to do, whose mockery
is turned back on herself. Live with your grief,
or your remorse. If ever I come to love you,
may Heaven wither the fresh shoots in my fields,
send my flocks straying, let them not find grass,
or rather, let them find it – poisoned. These
are the fruits of your own vanity. Enjoy them.
Shall I see you again? If ever I do,
may my eyes close in everlasting sleep.
Shall I speak to you again? If ever I do,
may my tongue burn with everlasting thirst.
And if I love you, if I feel myself
run mad for you again, may God himself
burn me to ashes with a thunderbolt.

(*He goes out.*)

ELISA: (*Alone.*)

Heaven pays no mind to the bragging oaths
of furious lovers – all gone, on the wind.
I trust my charms, weapons that rarely fail.
To all the creatures of the earth and sea,
Nature has given means for their defence.
She gave the tigress her rapacious claws,
the proud lion his strength, the bull his horns,
the horse its legs, the dog its teeth, the fish
its scales and gullet, the birds their beaks and feathers.
To men she gave reason, logic, and to women...?
Soft charms, sweet looks and floods of ready tears.

ACT FOUR

A room in the COMENDADOR's house, with a table laid.

(*At the start of the scene, the COMENDADOR, DONNA ANNA and DON JUAN are sitting at table. The SERVANTS, after clearing the table, except for the ornaments, leave.*)

DON JUAN:

Comendador, your courtesy increases
the weight of my already heavy chains.

COMENDADOR:

Your merit would demand a better welcome,
but more I cannot give, who have always been
an enemy to the heaping up of treasure.

DON JUAN: (*Looking at DONNA ANNA.*)

(Such beauty!)

DONNA ANNA:

           (What are they trying to say, those eyes,
which never leave my own? What is he thinking?)

PAGE: (*Entering.*)

Señor, by order of His Majesty,
Don Alfonso is below, and wants to speak
to you in private.

COMENDADOR:

           Send the servants down.

(*The PAGE leaves.*)

I must go down. Don Juan, you will forgive me...

DON JUAN:

Please – do not vex yourself on my account.

COMENDADOR:

Daughter, stay with our guest till I return.

(*He puts on the sword which had been lying on the table and goes.*)

DON JUAN:

(If he would just not come back till tomorrow.)

DONNA ANNA:

(My heart is pounding.)

DON JUAN:

           Fairest Donna Anna,
chance has, at last, created an occasion
for me to talk to you at liberty.

DONNA ANNA:
Perhaps my father's presence, and his principles,
inhibit freedom of speech?
DON JUAN:
The father's age
is less kind to me than the daughter's youth.
Ah, Donna Anna!
DONNA ANNA:
You are sighing, Señor?
(I wish my father would come back!)
DON JUAN:
Believe me,
it was no idle wish to wander through
Castile that brought me here. Your beauty's fame
had fired my heart. That was my guiding star;
that was what gave my steps love, rule and purpose.
I came to see you, and in your fair eyes
I saw a splendour which mere words could not
sufficiently describe, which mere desire
could not imagine. One same moment was
enough to see you, and to sigh for love.
I burn now with a flame I cannot bear;
I ask for your compassion.
DONNA ANNA:
I confess,
your words, as unexpected as they are,
perhaps, sincere, surprise me. I am not
aware of any merit in me which
invites the applause of fame, nor would I seek it.
Beauty passes with the years, and I
value an honest heart above frail looks.
DON JUAN:
Ah! Sweet sincerity, how rare that is!
I love it, and have sought for it so often,
to no avail. How fortunate I am
if this loving heart of mine could hope
to have found in you that true fidelity,
so longed-for and so unattainable.
DONNA ANNA:
One faithful heart can learn it from another.

DON JUAN:

May my love hope for favour at your hands?

DONNA ANNA:

If it is begged within the bounds of honour,

I may, perhaps, not be indifferent.

DON JUAN:

I understand your meaning – a chaste marriage;

that is the right true end of my chaste love.

That hand I sigh for...

(*Trying to take DONNA ANNA's hand, which she withdraws.*)

DONNA ANNA:

          Let us talk of this

another time.

DON JUAN:

          Now that we have this time,

why wait for another?

DONNA ANNA:

          (Father does not come back –

and where are all the servants?)

DON JUAN:

          I can feel

my heart melt in sweet fire to look at you.

Pronounce the one word "Yes" that gives me life;

and take my hand in yours, as surety.

DONNA ANNA:

My father must know of it. On him my will

depends. I am engaged to be the wife

of Duke Octavio; I cannot break the knot

alone.

DON JUAN:

          Love can do anything for us;

and if you love me, dearest...

DONNA ANNA:

          What is it

you want of me?

DON JUAN:

          The present of your hand,

and afterwards your father shall be told.

All is allowed when we wish to establish
our happiness; and I despise these idle
useless conventions.
DONNA ANNA:
                              Do you dare to speak
to me like that? But that is a disgrace,
provoking, and deserving of, contempt.
DON JUAN:
Let me advise you; give me as a gift
what a more resolute heart might take by force.
DONNA ANNA:
Are you so impudent that you advance
under that flag of temerity?
DON JUAN:
                                   Yes, and you
resist in vain: what I desire from you
is your hand as a gift – or else this steel
will bring you death.
(*Grasping his dagger.*)
DONNA ANNA:
                         Ah, shameful treachery!...
Servants, father, can nobody hear me?...
DON JUAN:
Servants, father, and the gods themselves
you call in vain; if finally you do
not acquiesce to my demands, then I
shall sink this...
(*Rising.*)
DONNA ANNA: (*Rising to leave.*)
                         God in Heaven...
DON JUAN: (*Holding her by her dress.*)
                                   Olà! Stop there...!
DONNA ANNA:
You villain!
DON JUAN:
             I shall hurt you...
DONNA ANNA:
                         You are a devil!
What is this violence...?

DON JUAN: (*Seeing the COMENDADOR approaching, he
releases DONNA ANNA.*)

(Ah, I am discovered!

Now I must make my way out with my sword)

(*Taking cloak and sword.*)

COMENDADOR:

Don Juan, what is this?

DON JUAN:

Nothing. I entreat

your leave to go.

DONNA ANNA:

Father! This man is a horror!

My hand, the hand that's promised to another,

he tried to take by force. He threatened me.

He would have used his sword on me.

COMENDADOR:

You dare

betray the laws of hospitality?

Low creature, do you outrage and insult

all those who trust you? Leave us, leave my house.

A shame like this demands revenge in blood.

DONNA ANNA:

(I must get help! The servants!)

(*Exit.*)

DON JUAN:

Comendador,

your age alone renders you less than apt

for combats of this kind. Find whom you like

to represent you; as a gentleman,

I shall answer with my sword, I promise you,

upon my honour.

COMENDADOR:

Lying, perfidious man,

what honour?

DON JUAN:

Take care you do not rouse my anger.

COMENDADOR:

A criminal's anger's easily aroused.

DON JUAN:

Vengeance is even easier for me.

COMENDADOR:

I can hold back no longer. Draw your sword!

DON JUAN:

Rash old fool, you will regret this boldness.

COMENDADOR:

Come on!

DON JUAN:

I am your man.

(*They fight.*)

COMENDADOR:

Ah, I am hurt!

Come back, you savage... Ah, I can no more.

DON JUAN:

His blood is not a sight that stirs my pity.

He caused his own undoing – let him mourn it.

(*Exit.*)

COMENDADOR:

The vile brute has run away, the traitor,
nor can I follow him... oh God!... my legs will not
support me any more. I am failing... falling!
Oh, daughter, daughter, can you hear? Where are you?
Poor girl, who will look after you? My powers...
abandon me; my heart fails in my breast.
My limbs are shaking... they no longer bear
the weight of a fading life... I can no longer
distinguish objects... I am going... dying...

(*He falls dead.*)

DONNA ANNA: (*Entering with SERVANTS.*)

Father, I am here... Oh, Heavens! What do I see?
He is not breathing... He is already dead.
Where is the murderer? Cruel, pitiless,
what had the poor man done to you? Oh, Father,
let these tears be the first pledge of my pity;
but expect from me a merciless vendetta.
His Majesty cannot deny me justice.
Pick up the body, friends, take him away.

(*SERVANTS remove the body.*)

Whoever could have dreaded or suspected
so cruel a heart in that inhuman breast?
The sweetness of his gaze, that humble look,
covered a hideous soul. What more will he
attempt, the monster? If I were less strong,
what would become of me? Oh, holy honour,
how many enemies you have! Behind how many
insidious arguments do they mask themselves!
Dear Father, you commanded me to stay
behind with him! You offered him... But no,
I was too rash. At the first villainous words,
the first deceitful glance, I should have found
safety in flight.

DON ALFONSO: (*Entering, with DON OCTAVIO.*)

      Donn'Anna, who is it
has robbed you of a father, me of a friend?

DONNA ANNA:

    A vandal murdered him. You can still see
his blood spilt on the ground: I ask for vengeance.

DON ALFONSO:

    Who was my poor friend's murderer?

DONNA ANNA:

                   Don Juan.

DON OCTAVIO:

    There! Did I not say he was a villain?

DONNA ANNA:

    A guest in our house.

DON ALFONSO:

              Duke, I entrust you with
this criminal's arrest. Deliver him
into the King's hands, either alive or dead.

DON OCTAVIO:

    I shall see your orders carried out.

DON ALFONSO:

    It is not possible for me sufficiently
to express the grief I feel for you, Donn'Anna.
Reason, however, must apply a rein
to your afflictions. Death is the common lot.

Happy the man who makes a glorious end
to an upright life. If you have lost a father,
remember that in me you have another;
one who will give you such proofs of his love,
that you shall be content.

DONNA ANNA:

                        Let the first office
of your charity, Senor, be this; break off
this engagement which affords me nothing but
unhappiness; let the Duke get himself
another bride. He'll find no shortage of them.

DON ALFONSO:

If that is what you wish. But will you now
be living without company?

DONNA ANNA:

                        At this moment
I do not know the wishes of my heart.

DON ALFONSO:

I understand. When you have ceased to mourn,
you will be in a state to think more clearly.

DON OCTAVIO: (*Entering.*)

Senor, you hope in vain for the arrest
of Don Juan.

DONNA ANNA:

               Has the criminal escaped?

DON OCTAVIO:

No, but he has taken sanctuary
in the privileged precinct, where, by the command
of the King, the King's law does not run, the courtyard
in which your father's statue was erected,
and which His Majesty proclaimed a haven
for refugees and fugitives from justice.
Your father's effigy now protects his murderer –
what irony!

DON ALFONSO:

             Double the guards around the building.
The traitor will not be allowed to leave.
The King shall know of the crime. Now, Donna Anna,
dry your eyes for ever. Concentrate

solely upon your father's glorious deeds.
Let virtue be your comfort and your guide.
(*He goes out with DON OCTAVIO.*)
DONNA ANNA: (*Alone.*)
    Those who do not feel grief can well afford
to counsel pious calm to the afflicted.
Who is there understands as well as I
what I have suffered in my father's death?
Where is another love that can make up
for the bereavement of my father's love?
It is the sheerest folly if we hope
to find it in the hearts of faithless lovers.
Lovers do not love us, they love themselves;
they see themselves reflected in our eyes,
and as their pleasure fades, so does their love.
Merciful Gods, for the sake of that great soul
that was my father, aid me and defend
my heart from common, human misadventure.

ACT FIVE

A courtyard with several monuments, among them the statue of the COMENDADOR.

DON JUAN:

Oh cruel Fate, into what mortal danger
have you now led me? To what mournful end
have you reserved me? Women! Oh, what baleful
ascendancy your beauty works on men!
What malicious star wishes to see me
the slave of my ungovernable desires?
I cannot see a woman I do not burn for;
I cannot light a fire I do not douse.
Ah, Donna Anna, cruel! Either you should
never have met my gaze, or else you should
have been less severe in your rejection of me.
Proud women, you presume to enchain your lovers,
and then you laugh at their predicament,
and with impunity deny your charity
to those whose hearts you break. A savage usage!
But what is to become of me? My fault
is aggravated by her father's death.
The daughter will be wanting her revenge.
They will all wish my death. For the time being
this place affords me sanctuary; later
cunning or gold must find me a way out.

ELISA: (*Entering.*)

Despite your treachery, Don Juan, I am here.
Real love does not desert you in misfortune.

DON JUAN:

Well, in my present quandary I need
a little more than feminine emotion.

ELISA:

I can help you escape.

DON JUAN:

But how? (Oh chance!)

ELISA:

    Two of the guards outside the courtyard are
    cousins of mine... Their favour could assist
    our flight.

DON JUAN:

               Pray Heaven! (Time for flattery!)
    Exquisite girl, enchanting paragon
    of love sincere and of fidelity,
    I am yours, Fate wills me to be yours; yes, Fate –
    which has now twice elected you to be
    my merciful deliverer and guide.
    I do repent my base ingratitude.
    That stupid shepherd may say what he will:
    thus Heaven decides – Elisa is Don Juan's.
    (*DONNA ISABELLA enters unseen.*)

ELISA:

    Come then, let me have your hand in marriage.

DON JUAN:

    Ah, but we have no time to lose, my idol;
    we must hasten our escape. I shall be yours,
    I swear it, the moment I am at liberty.

DONNA ISABELLA:

    (Ah! Traitor!)

ELISA:

               Yes, I still want to believe
    the things you say, though I have been deceived.
    Come with me; my cousins will be loyal,
    and show us how to find the secret passage,
    which leads beyond the courtyard's outer walls.

DON JUAN:

    (If I escape, you've seen the last of me.)

DONNA ISABELLA:

    (The wretch shall not accomplish his design.)
    Don Juan Tenorio, may Heaven grant you
    peace in your love.

ELISA:

               Who is this person who
    is interrupting us at such a moment?

DON JUAN: (*To ELISA.*)

(A creature driven mad by his misfortunes;
he dreams a thousand fables; those who hear him,
find in him cause for laughter or contempt.)

DONNA ISABELLA:

My dear girl, if you wish to know my state
I am the one to ask. I am a woman,
betrayed by the criminal who is with you now.

DON JUAN:

(Did I not say the creature was insane?)

DONNA ISABELLA:

The villain swore both love and faith to me;
then perjured himself and left me.

DON JUAN:

(Strange delusion!?)

DONNA ISABELLA:

Why not rather brag of having insulted
and scorned a simple girl? Heaven, in justice,
will give me my revenge.

ELISA:

(The way she talks
does not sound much like madness.)

DON JUAN:

(It is, I swear!
Let her run on; and let us go, my dearest,
to join our friends, who will soon open up
the way of our escape.)

DONNA ISABELLA:

Stop, wretch! If you
think to escape, by Heaven, you are deceived.

ELISA:

(I begin to have suspicions.)

DON JUAN:

(Damn this danger!
as fatal as it is unlooked for!) Come, Elisa.
(*He makes to go, but DONNA ISABELLA retains him.*)
Out of my way or I shall kill you.
(*Drawing his sword.*)

DONNA ISABELLA:

I

will sooner die than leave; you do not scare me.
(*She places herself* en garde.)

DON ALFONSO: (*Entering with GUARDS.*)

Put up at once! Would you be rash enough
to fight in the presence of the Royal Guards!
(*To the GUARDS.*)

Give up your swords.

DON JUAN:

(Lost!)

DONNA ISABELLA:

(When will my fortune change?)

Listen to me, Señor...

DON ALFONSO:

Another time.

DONNA ISABELLA:

(For the moment he cannot possibly escape.)
(*She leaves with ELISA.*)

DON JUAN:

(Now I have real need of ingenuity.)

DON ALFONSO:

As the man who made the false and boastful claim
to the honoured title of a nobleman,
the King will have your death at any price.
Hunger will kill you, if the sword does not.
There will be no one who will dare to feed you;
whoever dares, does so on pain of death.

DON JUAN:

Ah, just is the decree, I do confess
I have committed two crimes; both of them
call vengeance down on me; but if in pity
you deign to listen to me, you will find
the gravity of my faults diminishing.

DON ALFONSO:

Defend yourself then, if you can still find
reason to do so. What more can you say
after your confession of the facts?

DON JUAN:

> I say, Señor, the face of Donna Anna
> blinded me – seduced me; I took fire
> at those fair eyes, and to the fire of love
> was added an indulgence, as unwise
> as it was liberal, in the pleasures of
> the table; an intemperance – unworthy
> of a noble soul! Oh, the unhappy chalice
> of two perfidious gods, Cupid and Bacchus!
> I blush to tell you; but I must not hide
> the truth from you, for, at that fatal moment,
> so utterly did desire supplant my reason,
> I was no longer master of myself.
> Ah, what unlucky star compelled my host
> to quit the table, leaving me alone
> and ardent at the side of so much beauty?
> My burning heart interpreted the event
> prompted by its desires: I boldly asked
> the fair one for deliverance from my torment.
> She answered with contemptuous modesty;
> her rage lit up a further fire in me.
> Reason by now had fled me; and my fury
> carried me on to threats. At this sad juncture
> her father entered, armed, deaf to excuses –
> he challenged me. I, under provocation,
> gave blow for blow, governed not by my will,
> but by a cruel fate, which brought my sword
> fatally to his breast. He fell, transfixed.
> There, Señor, are my faults: I have confessed them.
> Remember, though, that I was blindly led
> by two blind, traitorous gods. If we could just
> free from this stone the fallen hero's voice,
> might it not plead for mercy for me now?
> Perhaps he now repents not having curbed
> his overpowering rage, perhaps he would
> condone in me a wild excess of youth.
> What use would my death be to him? What use
> my blood to his reluctant, grieving daughter?

To remedy his injuries, he should ask
for something else from me, something whose justice
I hardly could deny, my hand in marriage
to her who, through my fault, is now in mourning.
If Don Juan dies will Donna Anna's honour
be thereby restored? Will she allow
the world to harbour doubts of whether she
defended her honour from a resolute lover
successfully, or did she fight in vain?
Poor Donna Anna! Overborne by grief,
she does not see the greatest of her dangers.
I go too far – I know. The criminal
cannot prescribe the punishment for his crime.
However, is it not legitimate
to ask for pity, just as it is to make
such sacrifice as will restore the damage
without the loss of blood? Ah, Don Alfonso,
speak you for me. You can obtain for me
the royal clemency, and Donna Anna
will be rewarded with my hand, while you,
though losing one friend, will have gained another,
less valorous, I grant, but no less faithful.
Be my protector. Not from love of life
am I urged now to ask your charity,
but love of blood, and care for reputation.
The mercy of the great King of Castile
is known to all the world, as is his justice.
May he not now give an example of it,
which will both profit him and do him honour?
It is not the punishment of a crime for which
the world reserves its wonder, but the clemency
of a merciful monarch, since the world is full
of wretched crimes, but poor in merciful kings.

DON ALFONSO:
    Your plea for clemency's not all in vain.
    Nor do I refuse to intervene
    on your behalf before His Majesty.
    I will do, if the heart of Donna Anna
    may be appeased; but that will not be easy.

If you think she will accept in marriage
a hand still reeking with the blood of one
she loved so dearly, you deceive yourself.
And would you offer her a hand you have
already promised in marriage to another?

DON JUAN:

That is a promise which can be revoked
to save the honour of an injured woman.

DON ALFONSO:

Don Juan, the person who is laying claim
to the name of Isabella makes me fear
some intrigue on your part.

DON JUAN:

                     Señor, upon
the word of a gentleman, I do not lie.

DON ALFONSO:

I would like to think you would not wish to soil
the obligations of nobility.
I shall believe your words; however, if
they prove untrue, there will be no excuse
whatever that is able to redeem you
from the most ruthless punishment.

DON JUAN:

                     (A fate
from which I shall redeem myself by flight.)

DONNA ANNA: (*Entering in mourning.*)

Ah, Señor, my father's body has,
by force, been taken from before my eyes,
to be laid in the tomb; do not forbid
me now to shed tears by his monument.
Shade of my father... God! what do I see?
Don Juan – he's here? Ah, Don Alfonso, hear me:
in the name of my betrayed and murdered father,
let that inhuman creature there not come
to flaunt his crime before my face, unpunished,
or, carried away with anger, I may snatch
a weapon from the hand of one of the guards
and run the monster through.

DON JUAN:

(I hope in vain

for pity from that quarter.)
DON ALFONSO:

Donna Anna,

moderate your anger. It is for
the King to punish crimes, but he will not
punish them without a proper hearing.
Don Juan has asked for pardon; it depends
on you; if you will be content to hear him,
and if what he has to propose to you
is not entirely unacceptable,
then the King's clemency will not be wanting.
DONNA ANNA:

What can the wretched traitor say to me?
What can he propose that will not be
a machination of his savage heart?
DON JUAN:

Pity, Donna Anna, is what I ask.
I am at your feet; on you depends
my life no less than my dishonoured name.
You wish to see me dead? Here is my breast,
take a sword – run it through. You will the better
relieve your rage, and I at least shall die
without the shame of public punishment.
Remember it was love that blinded me,
and your fair eyes that first set me on fire,
and that to see you, to be near to you
alone and unobserved, and not to languish
and ask for charity would be impossible.
To a man driven desperate by your refusals,
who could apply a curb or give advice?
Your father challenged me at a sad juncture...
I can say nothing to excuse my crime.
I am guilty, I confess, and I should die.
You do not see me throw myself before you
to save my wretched life. Ah, all I ask,
for pity's sake, if pity is in your heart,
is that you show some scrap of kind regard,

if not to the life, at least then to the honour
of a lover who has been unfortunate.

DONNA ANNA:

Perfidy! You beg me for your honour;
what of *my* honour, which you tried to insult,
who will remove the stain of doubt from that?

DON JUAN:

I could restore it... Ah, no, I am mad!
I dream the impossible, and only add
new fire to your disdain.

DONNA ANNA:

Go on, continue:
What is your design?

DON JUAN:

To offer you
my hand in marriage.

DONNA ANNA:

Villain! Do you dare
to go thus far with me? And I permit it?
And you, Señor, how is it you oblige me
to listen to the accents of a traitor?

DON ALFONSO:

I only want an end to all this discord.

DON JUAN:

Oh, generous lady, piteous Donna Anna,
dedicate your anger to your father;
do not offer him the blood of a felon,
begging for pity. See these tears of mine,
wrung from my grief at seeing you in grief,
and from my knowledge that it is my fault,
and let them be the pledge of my repentance.
Oh, be not cruel...

(*He kneels.*)

DONNA ANNA:

You should abase yourself
not at a woman's feet, but at the King's.

DON JUAN:

Ah, no! I shall not get up from the ground,
until I hear my fate from your own lips:

pronounce my sentence, cruel one, pronounce it,
if you condemn me, I shall rest content.

DONNA ANNA:

I tell you, rise. (Alas! what strong enchantment
his words are working in my heart! So soon?)

DON JUAN:

(The cinders have begun to glow.) Come, spare
this trembling heart a future of suspense.
(*He rises.*)
Explain your cruelty to Don Alfonso.
I am ready to die, in any way you please.
Slake your heart's anger with my blood at least.
I ask but one thing from you, then I shall
go to my death content. Just look at me;
and for a moment suffer the sad gaze
of a man who dies for you. Could less be asked
of your charity by an unhappy man?

DONNA ANNA:

You ask me for a glance? And to what end?
Perhaps you hope, by means of lying sighs,
to weaken my resolve? (Ah, seeing him
humbling himself, with tears in his eyes,
makes coward of my anger!)

DON ALFONSO:

                      Donna Anna,
whence comes this new, strange change I see in you?
Is it pity? Is it shame? Contempt? Affection?
Tell me the truth.

DONNA ANNA:

                  Señor... the horror... I...
If I could... but no...

DON ALFONSO:

                  Enough, I understand you.
Compose these warring feelings in yourself.
Don Juan, your fate is still, for the time being,
held in the balance. Nor should you attempt
to hurry on what time may well improve.

DON JUAN:

Thanks to your kindness. (Night is coming on,
Elisa will be here, I shall escape.)

DONNA ANNA:

  (Shade of my father, you who haunt this place,
  forgive the shallow weakness of my heart.
  I am a woman, in the end...)

PAGE: (*Entering.*)

                   Señor,
  a messenger has delivered this – from Naples.

DON ALFONSO:

  See him looked after, and give me the letter.
  (*The PAGE leaves.*)

DON JUAN: (*To DONNA ANNA.*)

  I shall give you such proofs of my fidelity,
  they will quite cancel out my former error.

DON ALFONSO:

  (What do I read here? Treachery!)

DON JUAN:

                      (Alfonso
  appears disturbed.)

DON ALFONSO:

            (Perfidious deception!)

DON JUAN:

  (Alas! What is all this?)

DON ALFONSO:

                Hear me, Don Juan.
  The secretary to your King has written me
  this letter, at the King's request.

DON JUAN:

                 (Oh, God!)

DON ALFONSO: (*Reading.*)

  "Don Juan Tenorio, whose unbridled lust
  and treacherous heart have made him guilty of
  a thousand crimes, has lately fled the country,
  carrying off the heart of a noble lady –
  Donna Isabella, beloved only daughter
  of the unconquered Duke of Altomonte.
  She was betrayed, abandoned, and she now,
  in male disguise, pursues the vile creature,
  who is reported travelling to Castile,
  where he hopes to find asylum or escape.

Should these two subjects ever come within
the jurisdiction of your King, take care
of the offended lady; meanwhile send
the wretch to us in chains for punishment."

DONNA ANNA:

Heavens, what do I hear!

DON JUAN:

(This has undone me.)

DON ALFONSO:

What do you say, Don Juan?

DON JUAN:

That letter is
a pack of lies.

DON ALFONSO:

It does not lie. But you do.
You multiply your villainous deceits.
You say a madman is pursuing you,
who is not what he says, inventing falsehoods,
which you must pledge your honour to disprove?
What honour, wretched man, are you in a dream?
All has come out at last. The one who follows you,
whom you deceived, is Donna Isabella.
Unbridled lust and fury drove you on
to outrage Donna Anna. Inhuman rage
against her father gave power to your hand.
You will not be sent to your country bound in chains:
you will die here. Let the guards be doubled
about the courtyard. No one is to give
help to this criminal. I shall go myself
to hasten on the vengeance of my King.
(*He leaves.*)

DON JUAN:

Donn'Anna, show me pity!

DONNA ANNA:

Do you ask
for pity, who know no shred of it yourself?
I have allowed myself to be deceived
too long by your designs. I should have been
wretched indeed, had I assented to
the cruel plot your heart had laid against me?

What barbarous torments, what bleak destiny
had you in store for me? A gracious Heaven
came to my aid in time. Lift up your eyes
and rest them on my father's glorious image:
you tore the cruel wound in his breast,
and with that, crying aloud to Heaven for vengeance,
he will invoke the higher power of God.
(*She leaves.*)

DON JUAN:

Then must I die? And is there no more hope?
Perfidious stars, then let my life at least
be taken with a sword, that will cut off
both shame and grief in me.
(*CARINO enters.*)

                        Carino, come,
my shepherd friend. You can help me, bring me
the comfort I need in my last, fatal day.

CARINO:

You made the girl I loved unfaithful to me,
and in return, I am supposed to help you?

DON JUAN:

Revenge your wrongs. I am not asking you
for life, or liberty; I ask for death.
Kill me, in charity. I am so tired
of waiting for the final end of life.

CARINO:

Is this despair?

DON JUAN:

             It is; no more escape
for me. The gods are cruel, if they exist.

CARINO:

You must not speak like that. There is a God;
nor is He a tyrant. Turn to Him
with a humble heart, sincere prayers and vows,
and help will come.

DON JUAN:

             What Gods, what prayers, what vows?
What can I hope for from unheeding Heaven?
It is a long time since I lost the habit
of speaking to the gods.

CARINO:

(I am afraid.)

But in the state in which you find yourself,
constrain yourself to be yourself again.
Who can you hope for help from, if not God?
Repentance from the heart will be enough.
Don Juan, even if you are a gentleman,
do not despise a shepherd boy's advice.
Maybe this is the last time heavenly pity
will speak to you through me. Look up to Heaven...

DON JUAN:

Better I should invoke the horrid furies
of Hell, that they should come to tear my body.
For a man facing despair beyond all doubt
pity is useless, useless all advice.
I must die, but let Death come himself to fetch me.
What Fate reserved me for so harsh an end?
Cruel, barbarous mother, to give me life!
Unfeeling nurse, not to cut off that life
of treachery while I was in the cradle!
Oh, let me curse the day when I was born!
The vicious feelings nourished in my heart!
Donn'Anna, Elisa, Donna Isabella!
Which of you is it that will murder me?
Then do it, shepherd.

CARINO:

(This is horrible.)

Oh, calm that fury that has struck you blind;
come to yourself!

DON JUAN:

Here I am at my end;
disarmed, a captive, wracked with cruel hunger,
and crueller anger. Comendador, where are you?
Will you not take revenge for your own blood?
Will your fine effigy not fall on me,
and carry me down below the earth? Why not?
Could I, once more, before I die, transfix
that breast of yours! False, pitiless deities,
I defy the avenging power of your arm.
If it is true there is a Heaven above,

if there is justice there, then send the lightning
to strike me, kill me, bury me deep in Hell
for all eternity.

(A bolt of lightning strikes DON JUAN; the earth opens and engulfs him. CARINO dashes away in terror, then returns with the others.)

CARINO:

Help! Help! Oh! Help!

DONNA ISABELLA: (*To DON ALFONSO.*)

You hear the heavens, which that lying impostor
invites to strike at us.

DONNA ANNA:

Has Heaven perhaps
already chosen the victim of its power?

DON ALFONSO: (*To CARINO.*)

Where is Don Juan?

CARINO:

Far enough from here.

DON ALFONSO:

What? He's escaped?

CARINO:

If the Devil took him, he has.

DON ALFONSO:

What are you saying?

CARINO:

Ah! I can barely speak
for fright. He hurled such dreadful insults at
the Gods, the lightning came: it struck him,
the earth gaped wide, and he was seen no more.

DON ALFONSO:

The justice of a vengeful Heaven has
forestalled the tardy stroke of human justice.
Donna Isabella, you may now
return at your convenience to your country.
Your prayers were heard; your wrongs, you see, are righted.

DONNA ISABELLA:

No! It is not enough! This trivial comfort
is not sufficient to indemnify me
for my misfortunes.

DON OCTAVIO:

Donna Isabella,
I cannot now unfold the thoughts that press
upon my heart. Enough... in time I shall
be able to give vent to my affliction.

DONNA ISABELLA:

Your charity diminishes my sorrow.
Some consolation.

ELISA:

Let his punishments
be laid on thicker still. He has betrayed me:
and I call for vendetta.

CARINO:

Then you call
in vain; Heaven has done it for us all.

ELISA:

And you, Carino, will you be cruel to me?

CARINO:

And you can go as far away from me
as a hunted beast can travel in a day.
You have deceived me twice. You'll not succeed
a third time.

ELISA:

But I swear...

CARINO:

Just hold your tongue!
I know your swears – just let that be enough.

DON ALFONSO:

Do not complain of him, but of yourself;
you made yourself unworthy of his love.

ELISA:

I am not going to die of grief for that:
the girl who wants for beauty, wants for lovers.

DON ALFONSO:

Go back to your woods, and do not come
spreading such passions among honest people.

ELISA:

Oh, yes, you townsfolk are all so discreet,
so innocent. I'll go back to my woods

to get myself away from these sad people
of so-called quality: no shepherd would
have ever seduced me like a wicked townsman.
I know our shepherds' hearts, and I can turn them
whichever way I please: I'm a past-mistress
in the art of making prisoners of them.
But townsfolk – oh dear me! they're all deceit!
The cunningest woman in the world would have
to yield the palm for lying to such lovers.

DON ALFONSO:

Who would believe that such corrupted customs
should have begun already to pervade
the countryside? Come, friends, and let us learn
a lesson from this terrible example,
that a man shall die even as he has lived,
that as he sows so shall he reap, that Heaven
with justice punishes impiety,
detests the dissolute and abhors a rake.

FRIENDS AND LOVERS

Il Vero Amico

(1751)

for
Jonny Phillips

CHARACTERS

TRIVELLINO,
(Trivella) a servant

FLORINDO,
friend and guest of Sebastian

STELLA,
(Beatrice) Sebastian's sister

SEBASTIAN,
(Lelio) engaged to Clara

CLARA,
(Rosaura) engaged to Sebastian

HERR MAYER,
(Ottavio) Clara's father

The action of the play takes place in Hamburg (Bologna) in the neighbouring apartments of Sebastian and Herr Mayer. For the renaming of characters and locations, see Introduction.

This translation was made for the Glasgow Citizens' Company and first performed by them at the Citizens' Theatre, Glasgow, on February 7th, 1986, in a production by Robert David MacDonald, designed by Kenny Miller, with the following cast:

TRIVELLINO, Rupert Farley

FLORINDO, Jonathan Phillips

STELLA, Kate Kitovitz

SEBASTIAN, Dominic Arnold

CLARA, Anne Lambton

HERR MAYER, Giles Havergal

ACT ONE

Scene 1

SEBASTIAN's apartment.

(*FLORINDO pacing up and down in some agitation.*)

FLORINDO: Courage is all one needs – and resolution. These two passions must be treated in different ways. Friendship must be cultivated with all possible delicacy, love uprooted with all possible force. Trivellino! See my bags are packed and get a place on the coach for noon.

TRIVELLINO: Where for? If one may enquire?

FLORINDO: I am going back to Venice.

TRIVELLINO: So suddenly? Has something happened?

FLORINDO: Trivellino, time is passing, and I really cannot waste it in making you party to my reasons. Just go and order the coach.

TRIVELLINO: Do your hosts know you're leaving?

FLORINDO: They do not. I shall say a letter from my uncle obliges me to leave at once.

TRIVELLINO: The Signora Stella will be very upset...

FLORINDO: The Signora Stella deserves every respect as Sebastian's sister, but...

TRIVELLINO: And Signor Sebastian will be even more disappointed...

FLORINDO: However much I might wish to stay here, it is no longer possible. Go and order the carriage.

TRIVELLINO: At least wait until Signor Sebastian gets home.

FLORINDO: Has he gone out already?

TRIVELLINO: I heard them say he's gone to the Signora Clara's – about a ring.

FLORINDO: Hurry, to the post, or noon will be upon us.

TRIVELLINO: It's not gone nine yet. If you like, I could go and find Signor Sebastian at Signora Clara's apartment.

FLORINDO: Yes... no – he will be back.

TRIVELLINO: And if not? Could you go without saying goodbye to him.

FLORINDO: If necessary. I shall send to call him.

TRIVELLINO: Could you not go yourself? You are welcome enough at Signora Clara's.

FLORINDO: No time.

TRIVELLINO: The lady has shown you considerable attention.

FLORINDO: For heaven's sake, stop tormenting me.

TRIVELLINO: What do you mean?

FLORINDO: The carriage, for pity's sake.

TRIVELLINO: Are you feeling all right, Signore? You've gone all colours. Was it my mentioning Signora Clara?

FLORINDO: The carriage!

TRIVELLINO: Excuse me.

FLORINDO: Where are you going?

TRIVELLINO: To book the carriage.

FLORINDO: Come here.

TRIVELLINO: Signore?

FLORINDO: If you see Signor Sebastian, would you tell him I'm leaving?

TRIVELLINO: Signore.

FLORINDO: Where shall you look for him?

TRIVELLINO: At his fiancée's.

FLORINDO: Signora Clara?

TRIVELLINO: Signora Clara.

FLORINDO: Present my compliments to her as well. If you see her.

TRIVELLINO: Shall I say you're leaving?

FLORINDO: No.

TRIVELLINO: No?

FLORINDO: Yes, yes...

TRIVELLINO: Which?

FLORINDO: Neither.

TRIVELLINO: You want to go without her knowing?

FLORINDO: What I want... Here is the Signora Stella coming. Run along. No, stay.

TRIVELLINO: Don't you want the carriage?

FLORINDO: Yes, yes, the carriage.

TRIVELLINO: But if...

FLORINDO: Be off now, don't torment me.

(*TRIVELLINO leaves.*)

STELLA: Good morning, Florindo.

FLORINDO: Stella, I was hoping I'd see you.

STELLA: Why was that?

FLORINDO: To apologise for the long inconvenience I have caused you, to thank you for your untiring hospitality, and to ask if you have any commands for Venice.

STELLA: Venice? When?

FLORINDO: I am leaving. Immediately. I have just sent to order the carriage at the post.

STELLA: You're not serious.

FLORINDO: Never more so.

STELLA: But why?

FLORINDO: A letter from my uncle.

STELLA: Does my brother know?

FLORINDO: Not yet.

STELLA: He won't let you go.

FLORINDO: I hope he will not try to prevent me.

STELLA: He most assuredly will. And if he does not, I shall.

FLORINDO: Why should you wish to detain me?

STELLA: Before you go, give back what you stole from me.

FLORINDO: I have stolen something of yours?

STELLA: You have indeed.

FLORINDO: Really? Tell me what?

STELLA: I blush to admit it.

FLORINDO: If I am the thief, I should be the one to blush.

STELLA: My heart.

FLORINDO: It is a relief to know that such a theft is no crime of mine.

STELLA: No?

FLORINDO: There is no crime where there is no bad intention. And consequently there should be no punishment.

STELLA: If you have not wished for my heart, I cannot say the same for myself.

FLORINDO: Come now, let us act for the better for both of us. Take back your heart, and leave me mine. You will stay here, I will go to Venice, and heaven knows whether we shall ever see each other again.

STELLA: My heart will not change. Never.

FLORINDO: You do me an honour I do not, cannot deserve.

STELLA: But which obliges you to a reply.

FLORINDO: Which I find difficult.

STELLA: Signore, you are obliged.

FLORINDO: Tell me why.

STELLA: If a woman conquers shame to the extent of confessing her love, she does not deserve to be sent packing like a servant.

FLORINDO: It was not I who obliged you to speak out.

STELLA: I have been silent a whole month now.

FLORINDO: Had you been silent a month and a day, no harm would have been done.

STELLA: I am not sorry for what I said.

FLORINDO: I leave tomorrow.

STELLA: Here is my brother. (*SEBASTIAN enters.*)

FLORINDO: In good time. The sooner I say goodbye, the sooner I shall be gone.

SEBASTIAN: Friend, I understand from Trivellino you wish to leave. Is that true?

FLORINDO: Sebastian, if you love me, let me go.

SEBASTIAN: I should love you but little were I to refuse. I don't know what to say. I suppose I must agree.

STELLA: Are you so weak? You know why he's leaving? For a mere politeness. He told me: I have been a guest here for a month, it is time I relieved you of the burden of my company. Ehi. Friends do not behave like that. Two months, four, a year – you are master in our house, aren't you?

SEBASTIAN: That is true, Florindo, you are the master here. So do not insult me by supposing you are a burden. I'm not shy of saying so, you see.

FLORINDO: I do see, I know very well, but...

STELLA: Make him tell you why.

SEBASTIAN: Why, then?

FLORINDO: My uncle is extremely ill, and I wish to return to Venice before he dies.

SEBASTIAN: I cannot argue with that.

STELLA: There is one lie. He told me it was a letter from his uncle, and now he says his uncle is on his deathbed.

FLORINDO: I should have said it was a letter regarding my uncle...

STELLA: Don't change your cards in mid-hand.

FLORINDO: I assure you it is the truth.

STELLA: Show us the letter, and we shall know the truth.

FLORINDO: Sebastian will believe me without having to see the letter.

STELLA: You see what a liar he is? You see? He wants to leave because he is bored with us.

SEBASTIAN: *Lieber Freund*, is that possible?

FLORINDO: You wrong me to think such a thing.

STELLA: Florindo, I hope you will come and see me before you leave. I have to ask your assistance in a business at Venice.

FLORINDO: I shall be happy to receive your commands. (*Exit STELLA.*) It will be a token of your friendship if you will let me go without further attempts to prevent me.

SEBASTIAN: If that is what you want. Do me one favour though.

FLORINDO: Well?

SEBASTIAN: Wait until tomorrow.

FLORINDO: I should rather leave today.

SEBASTIAN: No, tomorrow. Today I need you.

FLORINDO: For what?

SEBASTIAN: You know I am engaged to marry Clara? Well, you do know, don't you?

FLORINDO: Yes. I know.

SEBASTIAN: You also know the shaky condition of our family finances. I hope to set all to rights with Clara's dowry; 20,000 marks her father has promised. But apart from that, she is a girl of great beauty and grace. Well, don't you agree? Is she not particularly fine? Intelligent? What is the matter? Don't you approve of her? Don't you find her beautiful?

FLORINDO: Yes. She is. Beautiful.

SEBASTIAN: She seemed to be in love with me, and for a while, I thought she was satisfied with me. But for some time now she has changed towards me, she no longer speaks so warmly, indeed she treats me with considerable coolness. I have tried to force the cause of this from her, but to no avail. I have gone so far as to suggest that if she has repented of our engagement, we are still in time to tear up the contract.

FLORINDO: What did she say to that?

SEBASTIAN: That the marriage had been arranged by her father, that she had no authority to cancel it, and that if it was I that was dissatisfied, then I should say so.

FLORINDO: That sounds like a modest well brought-up girl.

SEBASTIAN: Exactly, a modest well brought-up girl who does not love me.

FLORINDO: Oh, come now, it just seems like that to you. Women are subject to these minor vagaries just like anyone else.

SEBASTIAN: Women are changeable.

FLORINDO: And what about the rest of us? Have you never found yourself in her presence and with no desire to speak to her? Why should you imagine a girl always has to be of one mind? Would you wish her to laugh when she does not feel like doing so?

SEBASTIAN: Well, then, you go to see her. Bring the talk round to me...

FLORINDO: Sebastian, please – reckon without me in this. I have no wish to see the Signora Clara.

SEBASTIAN: What is this? Are you going to leave without taking farewell of a house where you have been received in conversation every day? Clara's father is your friend.

FLORINDO: I really have a great deal to see to; I beg you to make my farewells for me.

SEBASTIAN: But if you're not leaving till tomorrow, you can make them yourself.

FLORINDO: No. I must leave at once.

SEBASTIAN: You promised.

FLORINDO: Then I shall stay here with you, but I have no wish to socialise.

SEBASTIAN: Is there some mystery makes you unwilling to see Clara?

FLORINDO: What the devil do you mean? I am a man of
  honour...

SEBASTIAN: I meant you might have received some slight
  from her father. Squalid old miser, he would not hesitate
  to slight a friend for the meanest economy.

FLORINDO: Perhaps, but he is an old man, he has nothing
  in the world but his daughter, and if he makes economies,
  he makes them for you.

SEBASTIAN: But if he has put some slight upon you, I want
  to know. I should take it as a personal affront.

FLORINDO: No, no, he has done nothing.

SEBASTIAN: Then let us go and visit him.

FLORINDO: No, please, if you love me...

SEBASTIAN: Then it is Clara who has displeased you.

FLORINDO: She is incapable of displeasing anyone.

SEBASTIAN: Then you can have no reason to refuse.
  Come on.

FLORINDO: No, Sebastian...

SEBASTIAN: Friend, if you go on refusing me, I shall
  begin to suspect something worse. What is your answer?

FLORINDO: I do not wish to discuss it now. I will go
  wherever you wish.

SEBASTIAN: Let us go then. I want you to use your skill
  to raise Clara's spirits: bring the conversation round to
  me, and, if she has formed some bad impression of me,
  try to disabuse her. But if she has decided not to love me,
  I would like you to say, on my behalf, that a person who
  does not love me, does not deserve me.

FLORINDO: I am not good at that sort of thing.

SEBASTIAN: I know how expert you are in such situations.
  I have no friend I can trust as I do you. You owe me this
  favour before leaving: I can't believe you would want to
  leave me thinking you were no longer my friend.

FLORINDO: Whatever you wish.

SEBASTIAN: I shall go up with you, then leave you to your
  discussion. I expect you to bring me comfort and counsel.
  According to your report of her, I shall either leave off
  loving her altogether, or hasten on my marriage.

Scene 2

HERR MAYER's apartment.

HERR MAYER: This bit of paper will come in handy. Here's a bit of string will do to tie up... If I didn't concern myself with everything... they'd let the house go to rack and ruin. (*TRIVELLINO passes through with eggs and shopping bags.*) Gently, gently, wretched boy, you'll break them.

TRIVELLINO: Let me get them to the kitchen, so we don't waste the fire.

HERR MAYER: Who ordered it lit so early? I put it out; you can light it afresh. If someone didn't introduce some little economies, we would not be eating as we do. Come here. Did you shop well?

TRIVELLINO: I went half over town to get eggs at a pfennig apiece.

HERR MAYER: Terrible. Everything's dear, dear, dear. Life is impossible. How many did you get?

TRIVELLINO: Eight.

HERR MAYER: Eight pfennigs? What the devil do we need with eight eggs?

TRIVELLINO: For four people?

HERR MAYER: One person one egg, and not a bite more.

TRIVELLINO: What's wrong with putting the others in the larder?

HERR MAYER: They might fall, they might break – that damned cat...

TRIVELLINO: Put them in a crock?

HERR MAYER: And if the crock should break? No, no, put them in the flour bin, they'll come to no harm there. Show me. You fool. You have no idea how to shop. Imperceptible to the naked eye. Take them back.

TRIVELLINO: Biggest to be found.

HERR MAYER: Biggest? Biggest? Hahaha. Brainless oaf! (*Produces something like a lorgnette, but without a lens.*) This is the size of an egg. The ones that pass through this ring are too small; I don't want them. This one goes through, this not, that not, this yes, this yes, this not, this yes, that not. Keep these, and take the rest back.

TRIVELLINO: How am I supposed to find the peasant woman who sold them to me?

HERR MAYER: That is your worry. But how are you going to carry them? Not in your hand, you'll break them. Put them in the basket.

TRIVELLINO: There's other things in the basket.

HERR MAYER: Such as?

TRIVELLINO: Lettuce.

HERR MAYER: Ah, yes, lettuce, how much?

TRIVELLINO: Two pfennigs.

HERR MAYER: Half would have been enough. Take the other half back.

TRIVELLINO: How am I supposed to take back half a lettuce?

HERR MAYER: Give me the half in my handkerchief. (*Eggs fall and break.*) Oh, oh, oh, are you laughing, rapscallion? Laughing at your master's misfortunes? Very short-sighted of you.

TRIVELLINO: Signore, do not weep for the loss of two eggs.

HERR MAYER: No, for the loss of two pfennigs. Are you aware just what two pfennigs are? Money breeds, and to a man of judgement one pfennig produces more, as the grains in an ear of corn produce a sheaf.

TRIVELLINO: Do I still have to take these back?

HERR MAYER: No, I must eat them now, to my misfortune.

TRIVELLINO: I'll see to the fire.

HERR MAYER: Not too much wood, mind.

TRIVELLINO: To cook four eggs?

HERR MAYER: Four and four make eight. No comfort in this house. My daughter in love and thinking of nothing but getting married: and I must cut out a piece of my heart and pay over a dowry for the privilege, from the money I have brought together with such sweat and toil. Where are the good old days when fathers sold off their daughters? And the more beautiful they were, the more dearly the husbands paid for them. Clara's beauty would have brought me a fortune; but nowadays it is my most fatal misfortune. If I do not marry her off soon there will be trouble indeed. And I must rid myself of the incidental expenses. So many fashions, so many dresses, it can't go on. I shall make the effort, I shall marry her off. Poor treasure, gelded, gelded is what you will be. Here she is now. Some fresh demand on my wretched exchequer, I expect.

CLARA: Good day, *Vati*.

HERR MAYER: Ah, daughter, good days are for me a thing of the past.

CLARA: Now why should that be?

HERR MAYER: Because they do not bring in a single sou. Every new day it is spend, spend, spend, and we are on the road to ruin.

CLARA: Oh, come, the whole town knows you for a rich man.

HERR MAYER: Rich? Rich? Heaven blister the tongue of whoever speaks so ill of me.

CLARA: Saying you are rich is hardly speaking ill of you.

HERR MAYER: It could not possibly be more so. I shall no longer be safe in my own house. Thieves will break in. We shall be murdered in our beds. I must fit double locks, padlocks, bolts, bars, a portcullis.

CLARA: To hear you, one would think we lived in abject poverty.

HERR MAYER: All too true.

CLARA: Then how do you propose to marry me off with a dowry?

HERR MAYER: I lie awake nights thinking of nothing else.

CLARA: It is fixed at 20,000 marks.

HERR MAYER: Aie! Be quiet. Do you want to kill me?

CLARA: May heaven spare you these many years, but after your death I shall be your sole heir.

HERR MAYER: Heir? To what? What can you hope to inherit? To scrape together 20,000 marks I shall be obliged to sell everything and mortgage the remainder. I shall be a pauper, I shall beg alms by the wayside. My poor girl, if you hope to inherit anything, pray for your old father's speedy demise, kill him yourself. Oh, fatherhood, fatherhood, wretched condition. If the fathers are poor, the children do not realise the streams of gold that must be squandered to free themselves of the obligation of maintaining them; if they are rich, the children long for nothing but their death and the hope of inheritance. I am destitute. Clara, I have nothing; hope for nothing at my death, I swear it.

CLARA: Then what is in that safe in the wall of your room, which you keep locked with three keys and visit half a dozen times a day?

HERR MAYER: Safe? Safe? What safe? Just an old-fashioned closet... Three keys? It is open all the time... visit it half a dozen...? Oh, the malice of mankind. And womankind, always thinking the worse. I keep my handkerchiefs in it, my few poor tattered shirts, and other things I cannot mention, things I have need of in my old age. Safe? Money? For the Love of Heaven, girl, say nothing of the kind to a living soul. No safe. No money. Lies, lies, lies. (*Exit.*)

CLARA: Poor old man. Can he think I know nothing? There is money in that safe, a great deal of money, and at his death it will all be mine. But, oh, my happiness does not depend on money, but on the peace of my heart. Am I going to find that with Sebastian? For a time I acquiesced in loving him, and now I find I could almost hate him. But why? Why? Why such a change of heart? Florindo. Yes, there is the reason for this remarkable mutation. We have known one another a month, and every day I take fire further. All other objects have become odious, and most odious of all has he become who sought to engage my affections. Oh, Sebastian, once my hope, now my torment.

TRIVELLINO: Signora.

CLARA: What do you want?

TRIVELLINO: The Signor Florindo.

CLARA: What of him?

TRIVELLINO: He has called.

CLARA: Alone?

TRIVELLINO: The Signor Sebastian brought him to the door, then left.

CLARA: Quickly, quickly, show him in.

TRIVELLINO: He is in the next room talking with your father.

CLARA: Ah, yes, my father likes him: he brings him little presents.

TRIVELLINO: I just heard him asking Signor Florindo to send two pairs of spectacles and a jar of mustard from Venice.

CLARA: What do you mean? Venice? Is Signor Florindo leaving?

TRIVELLINO: What is the matter, Signora, you seem upset. Signor Florindo is a young man of infinite address, and shows himself most attentive. There is a certain sharpness in Signor Sebastian's manner which does not entirely recommend itself, and I can only add that, compared to the Signor Florindo, his purse strings are tied considerably tighter.

CLARA: It is undeniable the Signor Florindo has the most winning manners.

TRIVELLINO: Does his regard for you extend beyond mere politeness?

CLARA: How can I tell? He is certainly wondrously civil to me, but I would be loth to mistake mere good breeding for... anything else.

TRIVELLINO: Before he leaves, say something to him.

CLARA: Too late, too late, saddest words in any language.

TRIVELLINO: There is still time.

CLARA: Time wasted if he is leaving.

TRIVELLINO: Were you to say the right things, he might not leave.

CLARA: Oh, God! Here he is. (*FLORINDO enters.*)

TRIVELLINO: Come, compose yourself.

CLARA: No, listen...

FLORINDO: My humble duty to the Signora Clara.

CLARA: Won't you sit down? What is it, Signore? You seem in some unease.

FLORINDO: I received a letter from home, which has upset me somewhat. My uncle is on the point of death: I shall have to leave tomorrow morning.

CLARA: Tomorrow morning?

FLORINDO: Without fail.

CLARA: Tomorrow morning.

FLORINDO: Tomorrow morning.

CLARA: Poor old man, I feel for him. My father, too, is considerably advanced in years, and when I hear of old men dying, I can do no less than weep.

FLORINDO: You have a tender heart.

CLARA: And how is yours?

FLORINDO: So, so. Soft-boiled.

CLARA: So you leave here with no regrets?

FLORINDO: Ah, that far, alas, I cannot follow you.

CLARA: Your heart has attachments in this city, then, which make your parting bitter?

FLORINDO: I have never suffered in my life as much as I foresee I shall do tomorrow.

CLARA: Tell me with whom you leave your heart on departing?

FLORINDO: With a dear and true friend, whom I love as my other self.

CLARA: You love this... friend so much then?

FLORINDO: Those are the laws of friendship.

CLARA: And do you love none other than...

FLORINDO: I love all those who love Sebastian, and who are loved by him. That is why I can love...

CLARA: Me?

FLORINDO: Certainly. You are loved by Sebastian – you love him.

CLARA: How can you be so sure?

FLORINDO: Are you not to marry him?

CLARA: Things are not come to that yet.

FLORINDO: But they shall.

CLARA: And if they did not, would you not love me any more?

FLORINDO: I should no longer be obliged to by friendship.

CLARA: And were Sebastian to hate me, would you hate me too?

FLORINDO: Hate you?

CLARA: Yes, this great friendship you profess for Sebastian, would it oblige you to hate me?

FLORINDO: I could not do that.

CLARA: If you could not hate me out of friendship, then it cannot be out of friendship that you love me. I must therefore conclude, either that you are lying when you say you love me, or that you love me for some other reason.

FLORINDO: A clever woman can easily confound a man. I would only say the laws of friendship bind a man to stand to his friend in virtues, not in vices. As long as Sebastian loves with an honest heart, I am obliged to second that love. If Sebastian hated you, it would not be for me to foment that hate. I should endeavour to disabuse him, to bring him to a recognition of your merits, and do all I could to convert his feelings into love.

CLARA: You would have me Sebastian's, at any event.

FLORINDO: If I do, it is merely seconding his own intentions.

CLARA: And what of my own intentions?

FLORINDO: From the day I had the honour of meeting you, you told me you were in love with him.

CLARA: Since when a month has gone by.

FLORINDO: Has your opinion changed? Forgive me, dearest Signora – to crown your virtues, you need only the addition of constancy.

CLARA: Oh, Florindo, we are not always mistresses of ourselves.

FLORINDO: Signora, I leave tomorrow. I must thank you for the courtesies you have seen fit to show me, and since you display such kindness towards me, may I beg a favour?

CLARA: Heaven grant I can oblige you.

FLORINDO: Be kind to Sebastian.

CLARA: I thought you might ask something for yourself.

FLORINDO: But I do. I ask you to love me.

CLARA: Oh, heavens, is that the truth?

FLORINDO: Yes. I am asking you to love Sebastian, which is the same as loving me. My heart stays here with him, and if he has in any way diminished your good opinion of him, I implore you to pity him and love him.

TRIVELLINO: (*Enters.*) Signora, the Signor Sebastian is below.

FLORINDO: (Not before time.)

CLARA: Here is your heart. Receive it with the courtesy it deserves. I shall withdraw.

FLORINDO: Running away? From Sebastian?

CLARA: From Sebastian, from you, from two hearts that are equally laying siege to me.

FLORINDO: From me as well?

CLARA: Yes, from you as well. Would to God I had done so sooner.

FLORINDO: But what have I done?

CLARA: All the ill you possibly could; you have made me wretched, you have... My poor Florindo, no blame attaches to you. I am wretched for your sake, but I forgive you. Go, just go.

FLORINDO: No, please, listen, don't go... (*Exit CLARA.*) Oh, I shall never see Venice alive. Was ever a case like mine? I am in love, and cannot say so; the lady loves me, we both know it, and must pretend not to understand one another. We are sentenced to die in torment without hope of remission.

Scene 3

SEBASTIAN's apartment.

SEBASTIAN: Well, *caro amico*, how did the business go?

FLORINDO: I have no idea.

SEBASTIAN: Have you not said anything?

FLORINDO: As for that, things are not good.

SEBASTIAN: Is it such a business to find out a woman's feelings? I turned to you because I respect you and love you. I might as easily have entrusted the affair to any other of my friends, who would not have hesitated to oblige me, if they had been in town.

FLORINDO: Do not rely on your youth and charm to come to terms with your bride, and do not be too accommodating in allowing every sort of person access to her. Women are flesh and blood like the rest of us, and there is no point expecting more from them than we are capable of ourselves. If you should find occasion to be alone with a young woman, what do you imagine your heart would suggest to you? People should not be put next door to temptation, and then asked to resist it. Put straw next to fire, and it will catch, and once caught it is no easy matter to put it out. Friends are few and far between, and even those few may not be proof against that infection. Women are susceptible, love is blind, occasion prompts and Nature does the rest. *Amico*, he that hath ears to hear, let him hear: he that hath judgement, let him use it. (*Exit SEBASTIAN.*) I do not know where I am any longer. The conversation with Clara has utterly confused me. I did not ask to go there – Sebastian forced me. I think Clara realised I love her, just as I understood her to have an inclination for me. We parted somewhat unceremoniously. I feel obliged to see her again before I go, but if I go back there, it will be worse than ever.

TRIVELLINO: (*Entering.*) Signore, a letter.

FLORINDO: Where from?

TRIVELLINO: I really couldn't say. From a woman, by the smell.

FLORINDO: Here. Clara Mayer! From her! My heart beats.

"*Dearest Florindo...*" Dearest? To me, "dearest"? The word brings me out in a cold sweat. "*Since you are determined on leaving...*" Alas, I do not know how to resist. Discretion: let us not allow passion to veil our sight. Read it as an act of pure curiosity – civility. "*Since you are determined on leaving dearest Florindo...*" Oh, curse that "dearest". I read below, yet my eyes fly up to that. "*Since you are determined on leaving, and you do not, or pretend you do not know the state in which you leave me...*" Certainly I pretend, but, oh, I do know. "*I am constrained to open my heart to you.*" Do so, then, but I have made my decision. "*You must know, dearest*

Florindo..." (Oh, that word again!) "*You must know...*" I can't
see to read any more. "*You must know, dearest Florindo...*"
Why cannot I just skip the word? "*Since I first saw you,
I have been on fire...*" She has been on fire, and I have been
burnt. "*... on fire with your deservings, and that without your
presence near I shall most certainly expire...*" And so shall I; no
matter if honour and friendship can be saved. "*Be moved to
compassion, dearest friend.*" Again. The word tortures me,
addressed to me by such a hand. I cannot go on. I cannot
read it. Tear it up. Rid myself of it. What have I done?
Tearing up a letter so full of kindness? Before finishing
it? Not to know what she said at the end? If I could
reassemble the pieces. "*Dearest Florindo...*" No!! No
more! I will not torture myself any longer. But what am
I thinking of? To leave without saying anything? It
would be too cowardly, too indiscreet. I must reply.
A few lines, well-considered. The matter is out, it is only
fitting we speak clearly. To make her repent this love
of hers, as I do mine. And if one day Sebastian should
see my letter? Then he will see how I was capable of
sacrificing my love, my heart, my life even. How can
I begin? "Dearest Clara...?? Hardly. If the word has the
effect on her it had on me, she will die on the spot.

TRIVELLINO: (*Running in.*) *Signore padrone...*

FLORINDO: What is it?

TRIVELLINO: Quickly, for the love of God. Signor
Sebastian has been attacked: he is in danger. Come and
help him, quickly.

FLORINDO: Where?

TRIVELLINO: Out in the street.

FLORINDO: At once. (*He rushes out.*)

TRIVELLINO: I hate to get involved in that sort of thing.
Better I go and finish the packing. Just as well he is not
leaving till tomorrow morning, I'll have a little more
time. Anyway, who knows whether he will actually leave,
or not? Men in love sail where the wind blows. (*Exit.*)

STELLA: (*Entering.*) Florindo still does not show his face.
Can he be indifferent to my love? Yet I have seen him

look at me with some attention. Has he no opinion of me? Yet he has addressed some kind words to me. Yes, and been happy to joke with me often enough, and now he behaves harshly, like this, to me? Is he to leave tomorrow? In my despite? What shall I do? The mere thought makes me shudder. What is this? Florindo's writing. "*Signora...*" Oh, heavens, who is he writing to? It is not finished. Jealousy consumes me. "*Unfortunately, I have inferred that you have a kindness for me. It is for this reason I have resolved to leave sooner than I intended, since, finding your own inclination similar to my own, I would no longer be able to behave towards you with indifference.*" Could this be addressed to me? Could he be in love with me, as I with him? No, what obstacle could there be to his unburdening his love and enjoying mine? This is to some other woman. How can I get at the mystery? "*My friend Sebastian has received me in his house, shared with me all the secrets of his heart. What would he say of me, were I to betray my friendship and his hospitality?*" Oh, heavens, it is me he is speaking of, he thinks if he took advantage of Sebastian's trust to lay siege to his sister's heart... no, my dearest, it is no bad action to love those who love you. No love is reprehensible that can end in a marriage to the liking of the friend himself. I see now why you refuse to have relations with me, you are afraid of displeasing my brother, 'betraying his hospitality'. "*You yourself feel it is not fitting that...*" There the letter ends: but there my hopes begin. "Not fitting..." But it *is* fitting to speak in good time, to reveal the secret, and mutually console our loving hearts. Here is my brother, most apropos. What? has some accident occurred?

(*SEBASTIAN enters, his head bandaged.*)

SEBASTIAN: I was playing faro this morning, and was cheated by a confidence trickster. I exposed the brute, he replied too boldly, I took him a cuff in the face, he joined with a companion, they followed me into the street, and attacked me. I defended myself as best I could, but they were two to one, and had Florindo not arrived in the very nick of time, I should have stayed in the street.

STELLA: Where is Florindo?

SEBASTIAN: Trivellino is looking after him.

STELLA: Is he hurt?

SEBASTIAN: Not a scratch. He knows how to take care of himself. He put the ruffians to flight.

STELLA: What a man!

SEBASTIAN: Yes, a man of singular merit.

STELLA: And a good friend to you.

SEBASTIAN: His friendship is of the rarest kind.

STELLA: Now see where his delicacy leads him. He is in love with me, and dares not declare himself, fearing that such a love might be a violation of hospitality.

SEBASTIAN: Sister, you flatter yourself entirely without foundation.

STELLA: I can give you proof.

SEBASTIAN: You have your points, but... what proof?

STELLA: Read this. From Florindo...

SEBASTIAN: To you?

STELLA: He had no time to finish it.

SEBASTIAN: Let me see. I understand. He is a man of delicacy. I shall talk to him, find out his intentions.

STELLA: Tell him not to leave.

SEBASTIAN: If it turns out he does love you, he will not leave.

STELLA: If it turns out? Do you doubt it? Is it so very strange a thing that I should be loved? You know yourself how many prospects I have entertained; but this one pleases me more than all. Poor Florindo. Go and console him: tell him he shall be contented, my hand shall be his, he is not to doubt, to sigh, I shall be his *cara sposa.* (*Exit.*)

SEBASTIAN: This all seems very strange; Florindo hiding his passion for fear of my displeasure. He must know I love him. But this is his writing. Stella says it was addressed to her: anyway, who else has he to write to? We have always been together. He has no affairs in the city. (*FLORINDO enters.*) Dear friend, let me embrace you once more: I owe you my life.

FLORINDO: My duty, no more.

SEBASTIAN: Had you not come, those villains would have overcome me. What are you looking for?

FLORINDO: Nothing, just a piece of paper.

SEBASTIAN: Paper?

FLORINDO: Yes, have you been in here long?

SEBASTIAN: Since I left you.

FLORINDO: Has anyone else been in the room?

SEBASTIAN: Are you looking for a letter?

FLORINDO: The draft of one.

SEBASTIAN: This?

FLORINDO: Sebastian, forgive me, one does not touch other people's correspondence.

SEBASTIAN: Nor did I have the temerity to.

FLORINDO: How does it come to be in your pocket then?

SEBASTIAN: By chance.

FLORINDO: Enough... I repeat... a draft... written on a whim.

SEBASTIAN: Perhaps... but, forgive me, a reasonable man like yourself does not ridicule an honest woman in that manner.

FLORINDO: You are right. I was wrong. I apologise.

SEBASTIAN: Let us not talk of it any more. Our friendship has no reason to founder on that.

FLORINDO: I should not like you to think I had written it out of inclination, passion.

SEBASTIAN: Dear friend, I know all, I know to whom this letter was addressed. I admire your delicacy, but you reckon ill of my friendship if you hide the secrets of your heart from me.

FLORINDO: You are entirely deceived...

SEBASTIAN: I am not. I compare the letter with previous conversations. You have hidden the truth from me, but since I have discovered it, I tell you, I consider myself fortunate, if it is in my power to make you happy.

FLORINDO: You would wish that?

SEBASTIAN: With all my heart. But even I can see that circumstances are opposed to it; I have understood from the beginning that you wrote it on a whim, and you are making fun of a woman who flatters herself.

FLORINDO: I cannot think she has any grounds to do that.

SEBASTIAN: Let me assure you she does so immoderately. You know how women are. The attentions of a civil fellow are interpreted as an inclination. And, to tell the truth, she herself has told me she reckoned highly on your inclination towards her.

FLORINDO: (*Startled.*) And what did you reply to that?

SEBASTIAN: That I thought it unlikely, but that I would speak to you, and if it should turn out that what she supposed was true, I would further her inclinations with the best will in the world... Tell me the truth: do you want to marry her?

FLORINDO: Oh, heavens! What are you asking? What a trial are you putting my sincerity to, my duty? I am not in a position to accept such a sacrifice.

SEBASTIAN: No, tell me, sincerely. Do you love her or do you not?

FLORINDO: I esteem her, I have every possible regard...

SEBASTIAN: And on account of this esteem and regard, you would marry her?

FLORINDO: Oh, God, I don't know, if it were not doing a wrong to you...

SEBASTIAN: Wrong? What wrong? Come now. You are afraid of offending hospitality with a sincere love, but you offend it far more by an obstinate silence. If you love me, admit the truth; if you persist in denial, you are no longer my friend.

FLORINDO: I can hardly resist such a challenge. Very well. I confess the truth. Love has wounded me, taking me unawares. You have been the innocent cause of my unhappiness, and, so as not to abuse your trust, I have decided to leave.

SEBASTIAN: But you stay until I have made your peace.

FLORINDO: How?

SEBASTIAN: In marriage with her who has wounded you.

FLORINDO: How...

SEBASTIAN: Absolutely. If you wish, she shall be your bride.

FLORINDO: Oh, God... Sebastian... my friend... I am beside myself...

SEBASTIAN: Why did you not tell me sooner?

FLORINDO: I had not the courage... how could I?... it did not seem a good action.

SEBASTIAN: Well, come now, you shall be content.

FLORINDO: My heart is... overflowing with joy.

SEBASTIAN: And mine. I can imagine no greater joy than to be able to call you brother.

FLORINDO: Brother?

SEBASTIAN: That is the normal title of the man who marries one's sister. What is the matter? You seem confused.

FLORINDO: (*Dashed.*) It is just – the effect of happiness.

SEBASTIAN: After all, Stella is by no means to be despised.

FLORINDO: No, no, by no means, she is very beautiful.

SEBASTIAN: When would you like the wedding to be?

FLORINDO: We can talk about it, we can talk about it.

SEBASTIAN: What on earth has possessed you?

FLORINDO: It is very hot.

SEBASTIAN: The fire of love?

FLORINDO: You know nothing of the fire that burns me; so you make fun of it.

SEBASTIAN: No, no, I sympathise. I shall hurry on the wedding as fast as I can. I shall go and see Stella now; if she has no objection I can give you her hand as soon as you wish.

FLORINDO: Dearest friend, one thing, I beg of you, speak of this to no one.

SEBASTIAN: Why ever not?

FLORINDO: I have my reasons. I have written nothing to Venice. My uncle might be displeased were he to hear from any mouth but mine. You know the fashionable appetite for gossip.

SEBASTIAN: My sister may not have much of a dowry, but our family is quite worthy...

FLORINDO: Yes, yes, everything will be all right. I had just rather no one knew of it yet.

SEBASTIAN: I shall not tell a soul.

FLORINDO: I trust you.

SEBASTIAN: I may tell Stella, I suppose.

FLORINDO: Not her neither.

SEBASTIAN: Heavens! Not tell the bride? Is it to come a surprise? When?

FLORINDO: If she knows, so will the whole town within twenty-four hours.

SEBASTIAN: Oh, now, this is too absurd. Cheer up, friend, look forward with me to the time when this marriage shall be concluded, when you will be happy, and contented. (*Exit.*)

FLORINDO: (*Alone.*) Fine happiness. Fine contentment. What is this trap I have fallen into? What must I do? Marry Stella? How can I? Refuse her? Sebastian will say I have jilted her, that I am mad. If I go, I do ill. If I remain, I do worse. And what will Clara say of me? I hope Sebastian will tell her nothing, but if he does? I have to undeceive her. But how? There are two things I have to do: talk to Clara, and leave this place. The first as an act of gratitude, the second to salvage a friendship. Oh, with these two butchers on either side of me, love on the one hand, friendship on the other, the two greatest virtues have become my two greatest torments.

Scene 4

HERR MAYER's apartment.

CLARA: Did you deliver that letter? Why does he not answer?

TRIVELLINO: No time?

CLARA: If he were to leave without answering?

TRIVELLINO: Equally possible. Those who fall in love with foreigners must expect these things.

CLARA: But how could he? He is too well-bred to do such a thing.

TRIVELLINO: And if he does answer, where's the good in that?

CLARA: It will be something.

HERR MAYER: Satan finds work for idle hands to do.

TRIVELLINO: (What's the old skinflint muttering about now?)

CLARA: (Will this torment ever end?)

HERR MAYER: A lady of leisure, I perceive. Leisure never paid the rent. (*Handing her a ledger.*) Here, take this and pass the time.

CLARA: Oh, really, Father, this is really most tedious.

HERR MAYER: And you, boy, if you have nothing to do for the other tenants in the other apartments, there is no need for you to wear out my carpets and distract my daughter. Are you aware that in the two years and a month you have been working in these apartments, you have consumed 2,283 bread rolls?

TRIVELLINO: Approximately, of course.

HERR MAYER: Good for nothing but eating and drinking, and a crass incompetent in all else.

CLARA: Oh come now, don't be on at him. That great lubberly oaf of a cook-boy is the one who does nothing in this apartment.

HERR MAYER: Lubberly oaf? Admirable youth. Best servant I ever had.

CLARA: And in what does his particular merit reside, pray?

HERR MAYER: I don't have to pay him a salary, he is happy with bread, wine and soup, and an egg every now and again, should any remain unbroken.

TRIVELLINO: If you won't pay him wages, he'll cheat you on the shopping.

HERR MAYER: Cheat me? Are you telling me he will steal from me? Is that possible? I'll send him packing.

CLARA: And who will look after you then, poor thing?

HERR MAYER: Do it myself, do it myself. And I can tell you one thing, I shan't be buying eggs that go through the ring. Oh, no, indeed.

TRIVELLINO: Miser!

HERR MAYER: Tcha! Sticks and stones. Anyone's poor, they say he's a miser. Run along, and tell the boy to sieve the bran, and make me a soup this evening with the separated flour, and two drops of oil.

TRIVELLINO: Was it soup you wanted, or glue?

HERR MAYER: Pouf! With the flour you use for powder in a year, you could make a whole bag of bread.

TRIVELLINO: And with all the grease on that coat, you could feed a family of fourteen.

HERR MAYER: Impertinent! Be off. I wish to talk to my daughter.

TRIVELLINO: Then I shall go and do something useful.

HERR MAYER: High time. What would that be?

TRIVELLINO: Pray heaven to take you off our hands as soon as possible. (*Exit.*)

HERR MAYER: Odious boy. Is that any way to speak to one's employer?

CLARA: Oh come, it was a joke. Nor are you his employer. He serves all the apartments here.

HERR MAYER: I've a mind to speak to the landlord.

CLARA: He's no great friend of ours since you accused his dog of doing all...

HERR MAYER: Yes, yes, never mind, never mind that. Daughter, I must talk to you on a matter of some importance. Tell me, now, do you love your old father?

CLARA: What a question.

HERR MAYER: Would you like to see him dead?

CLARA: Don't say such things.

HERR MAYER: Then you would not want to deprive me of all I have in the world.

CLARA: For goodness sake...

HERR MAYER: Such as the dowry left you by your mother.

CLARA: If you do not wish to give the dowry, then do not talk of marrying me off.

HERR MAYER: I shan't mention it again,

CLARA: But what about Sebastian? You have a contract.

HERR MAYER: If he will take you without a dowry, well and good. If not, we can tear up the contract.

CLARA: Then let us do just that. He will not want me without a dowry.

HERR MAYER: But hundreds of girls find husbands without a dowry. Why not you?

CLARA: Come now, I have no such great mind to marry.

HERR MAYER: But, Clara, my dearest child, I do not know nowadays how I shall be able to maintain you.

CLARA: Then I shall be happy to get married.

HERR MAYER: Good, good. But without a dowry.

CLARA: No one in town will take me.

HERR MAYER: That Venetian fellow seemed a gentlemanly sort of person.

CLARA: Signor Florindo is certainly a young man of great good breeding.

HERR MAYER: Always brings me something.

CLARA: And generous to a fault. He always brings something for Trivellino too.

HERR MAYER: For Trivellino. How much?

CLARA: Three marks so far.

HERR MAYER: Three mar... Well, he can whistle for his Christmas box. If this Signor Florindo is in love with you...

CLARA: What reason have we to suppose that he is any such thing?

HERR MAYER: ... I should have thought he could have sewn things up by now without this piddling business of a dowry. What on earth does he want with a dowry anyway? He's an only son, rich, generous. Tell me, Clara, would you take him?

CLARA: Ah, why not? But Sebastian?

HERR MAYER: Wants a dowry.

CLARA: Enough now, we'll talk about it.

HERR MAYER: I shan't rest easy till I know.

TRIVELLINO: (*Entering.*) Signora, the Signor Florindo asks whether you are receiving.

HERR MAYER: Talk of the devil. Come, bird, come.

CLARA: Show him up.

HERR MAYER: Here. Did he give you anything?

TRIVELLINO: Who wants to know?

HERR MAYER: I'll have it out of your wages.

TRIVELLINO: If you don't pay me, I'll get the money where I can.

HERR MAYER: What's that? Where?

TRIVELLINO: Out of your rotten safe. (*Exit.*)

HERR MAYER: Safe? What safe? I have no safe. A box full of rags, full of rags. Damn whoever calls it a safe, and damn me too if I have any money.

CLARA: Come on now, don't be in a taking.

HERR MAYER: That boy will be the death of me. Now, make yourself agreeable to Florindo. Find out whether he might have an inclination for you. Bid him have a word with me, and I can settle the business.

CLARA: And if he too requires a dowry?

HERR MAYER: Let him whistle for it.

CLARA: Don't you think you might put your hand into your safe?

HERR MAYER: May all the teeth fall out of the head of whoever said it was a safe. If you hope to get married with the dowry in my safe, you'll wait till donkeys fly. You know where my safe is? What it is? There, in front of me – you are it. I hope he'll marry you without a dowry, and take on my expenses into the bargain. (*Exit.*)

CLARA: (*Alone.*) My father makes himself miserable, and refuses me a dowry, but if this might serve to shipwreck my agreement with Sebastian, I shall not refuse to be a party to the arrangement. If fate does not intend me for Florindo, I have no mind to another.
(*Enter FLORINDO.*)

FLORINDO: Signora. You will say I am too bold, coming to incommode you twice in one day.

CLARA: You mortify me saying such things. Your visits are always dear to me, and now doubly so.

FLORINDO: I was in duty bound to answer your courteous letter.

CLARA: You make me ashamed, speaking so openly of my weakness.

FLORINDO: Why should you be ashamed of a passion expressed with such modesty?

CLARA: Signor Florindo, before we speak of anything else, are you still determined on leaving tomorrow?

FLORINDO: I must.

CLARA: But why?

FLORINDO: Because I do not want love to force me to betray friendship.

CLARA: Then you do love me.

FLORINDO: You have been kind enough to open your heart to me: I can do no less to you. Signora, I have loved you from the first day I saw you, and now more than ever.

CLARA: But you still have the heart to leave me?

FLORINDO: I must salvage decorum, and not expose myself to criticism and derision.

CLARA: But if there should be a safe and easy remedy, to ensure that Sebastian should renounce me, would you be in a position to accept my hand?

FLORINDO: It is superfluous to consider so remote a possibility.

CLARA: Sit down a moment.

FLORINDO: I should leave, Signora.

CLARA: I ask you one favour, can you refuse me? Sit down a minute, and listen to me, and then you shall leave. Let me tell you how things are in this household, and perhaps what seemed impossible to you will seem less so. My father, as you know, is... (*Enter SEBASTIAN.*)

SEBASTIAN: Ah, dear friend, how pleasant to find you here.

FLORINDO: I was here... I was looking for you, Sebastian, for you.

SEBASTIAN: So, stay where you are, don't move.

CLARA: It seems to display a certain degree of temerity to enter unannounced in this way.

SEBASTIAN: A liberty a bridegroom may surely take with his bride.

CLARA: A liberty which on occasion not even husbands should take with their wives.

SEBASTIAN: Husbands who are used to being dictated to.

FLORINDO: Forgive me if on my account...

SEBASTIAN: Not at all. I take Clara's reproofs for whims. Would you have any objection to my sitting down too?

CLARA: Our house is yours.

SEBASTIAN: Florindo and I are two friends who are like a single person.

CLARA: For you maybe, not for me.

SEBASTIAN: And now not only my friend, but my brother.

CLARA: Oh?

SEBASTIAN: He will very soon be marrying Stella.

CLARA: Signor, I am delighted for you.

FLORINDO: Sebastian is joking.

SEBASTIAN: No, no it is the truth.

CLARA: I am so glad.

FLORINDO: Don't believe him.

SEBASTIAN: Florindo, I am hardly violating your confidence by telling Clara. She is a woman of discretion, and since she is to be my wife, she has a right to know it.

CLARA: Ah, was I not supposed to know? Then you will not be leaving tomorrow?

SEBASTIAN: No indeed, he will not.

CLARA: Just that I was informed that he was.

FLORINDO: Reliably informed, Signora.

SEBASTIAN: Florindo, you make me laugh. In love with my sister a whole month, and it is only this morning you declare yourself, in a letter.

CLARA: A letter?

FLORINDO: For heaven's sake, don't believe a word of it.

SEBASTIAN: No, please, I should not like to pass for a liar with Clara. Here is the very letter. To my sister.

CLARA: I am so relieved.

FLORINDO: There is no mention of Stella's name in that letter.

CLARA: Oh, come now, Signor Florindo, do not be reluctant to admit the truth. After all, Stella is entirely worthy of you. I see from this letter you do really love her.

FLORINDO: That does not seem to me at all how the letter reads.

SEBASTIAN: Surely we can speak freely here. The three of us have the same interests at heart. No one shall know of it apart from ourselves. But don't make me out an idiot. You told me you were in love with my sister. You agreed we should arrange the wedding.

FLORINDO: I said we would talk about it.

CLARA: My dear Signor Florindo, that which you have to do, see you do it quickly.

FLORINDO: Please!

SEBASTIAN: I thought we might have a double wedding.

CLARA: Signor Florindo, even if you intend to wait to bestow your hand on Stella, until I give mine to Sebastian, I fear the impetuosity of your love will hardly allow you to. My father cannot give me a dowry, so I am now a poor woman: a marriage of that nature will hardly suit Herr Sebastian, nor his family, whose reproaches I do not wish to endure. So occupy your mind with concluding your own match, and do not concern yourself with mine. As for myself, I see now that Fortune is less than kind to me, that men despise me, and that, to complete my wretchedness, even those who set such a high price on their spotless honesty, now deem it a virtue to lie to me. (*Exit.*)

SEBASTIAN: Florindo, did you hear?

FLORINDO: I heard how you keep your word to me.

SEBASTIAN: But Clara does not count.

FLORINDO: When I told you to keep silent to everyone, I meant everyone. No, really, this has upset me.

SEBASTIAN: Please, I'm sorry, forgive me.

FLORINDO: Very well, we are friends, and there is nothing a friend may not be forgiven.

SEBASTIAN: I am so fortunate to have found one who can bear with my faults. But Florindo, did you not hear? Clara will have no dowry.

FLORINDO: A great misfortune for a girl.

SEBASTIAN: But what am I to do? Marry her or let her drop?

FLORINDO: I am no good at giving that sort of advice off the cuff.

SEBASTIAN: Oh, well, think about it at leisure. I'm going to have a word with her father, then I am all yours. Wait for me here, we can leave together. I will depend entirely on your advice. I love her, but I cannot afford to ruin myself. Think of it, and, if you love me, dispose me to do what you would do yourself in my position. I trust you. Absolutely. (*Exit.*)

FLORINDO: And this on top of all? Must I advise him in a matter whose outcome can only be to my disadvantage? If I tell him to marry her, I do two evils: to him, since because of me he will marry without a dowry, and to myself, since I shall lose all hope of Clara. If I advise him to drop her, I do three evils: to Sebastian, in depriving him of a girl he loves; to Clara, in preventing her from getting married; and to myself, since, even were I to marry her, Sebastian would accuse me of having advised him in order to get her for myself. What can I do? Oh, heavens, if there is any one standing in urgent need of enlightenment and advice, surely it is myself.

ACT TWO

Scene 1

The MAYER's apartment.

HERR MAYER: Nobody here to tease me. Don't want the
servants coming in on a pretext, of dusting or sweeping.
Bad enough they should have caught sight of the big safe,
where I keep the silver. I can't move that; it's built into
the wall. But after all, that's not where I keep my best
treasure, my great capital. (*He takes out a strongbox.*) Here is
my heart, my saint, here is my redemption, my darling,
my best beloved, my gold. Oh, my dear, let me look at
you. Let me restore myself, console myself, feed myself
with gazing at you. My bread, my wine, my body, my life,
my precious viands, my pastime, my conversation: let the
idle go to the theatres, to parties, to balls. When I see you,
I dance, I rejoice. Gold, life of man, succour of the poor,
support of the great, triumph and calamity of the human
heart. Ah, every time I open you, my heart pounds, for
fear some alien rapacious hand has violated you. Alas, my
dear one, for three days now, I have not added to you.
Poor dear. Do not think I have left off loving you. I think
of you waking, dream of you sleeping. To increase you,
dear store, is all my care. I risk my money at twenty per
cent; in less than ten years I shall give you a companion,
no less strong, no less full than you. Ah, if I could live
a thousand years, and every year bring you a new
companion, and in the midst of a thousand chests,
surrounded by you, my children, my children's children,
to die... Die? Must I die? Poor chest. Must I leave you?
Ah, I am in a sweat. Quickly, quickly, let me look at you
again, my gold, my consolation. I cannot go on. Ah, fair
coin of Portugal. How beautifully minted. I remember,
I made you from all that grain I hoarded during the
famine. All those unfortunates wailing because they had
no bread, and there was I laughing, raking in the
doubloons. And such beautiful gold marks, you could

have been minted yesterday. I took you from that eldest son, who sold an estate on his father's death to pay me back 100 mark capital. What an affair.

TRIVELLINO: (*In hiding.*) (The old monster! Look at all that.)

HERR MAYER: Ah! What was that? Is the roof falling in, the house falling about my ears? Oh, my dear, pray Heaven you will not be buried under the ruins. Who's there? Who is that? Quick! Quick! Poor me. There are people in the room. I'm going to be murdered! But there's nobody. Pouf, imagination, maggots only. My dearest gold...

TRIVELLINO: Hands off!

HERR MAYER: Who spoke? What? Where are you? Who are you?

TRIVELLINO: The Devil.

HERR MAYER: Ach... Ach... Hideous demon, what do you want with me? Ach, if you have come for me, take me, but leave my gold. Let me put it back. Let me shut it up again. I'm shaking. I need a drink of water. But I must put it back, make it safe. I can't... go on... Trivellino... No, he mustn't see it. I'll put it back first... I haven't the strength. I must try. Ah, demon, leave me my gold, let me enjoy her a little longer. Don't part us now. There. All safe. Now for a drink, after the fright I've had. Is it well covered? Can people see it? Better I stay here. But I must take a tablet... I shall go and come back. Be quick. Two sips and I'll be back. Help! The Devil!

SEBASTIAN: (*Enters.*) Herr Mayer, what is the matter?

HERR MAYER: What are you doing?

SEBASTIAN: Coming to speak to you.

HERR MAYER: Go away: I can receive no one.

SEBASTIAN: Two words only.

HERR MAYER: Quick then.

SEBASTIAN: But what is wrong?

HERR MAYER: I was frightened.

SEBASTIAN: What of?

HERR MAYER: I don't know.

SEBASTIAN: Have a glass of water.

HERR MAYER: Yes, let us go.

SEBASTIAN: I shall wait for you here.

HERR MAYER: No, sir. You come too.

SEBASTIAN: I have to speak to you in private.

HERR MAYER: Speak then.

SEBASTIAN: Go and get your glass of water. Shall I call the servants?

HERR MAYER: No! I feel a little better. Say what you have to say.

SEBASTIAN: Very well. As you know, I am engaged to your daughter.

HERR MAYER: Water! I can't go on.

SEBASTIAN: But there are certain difficulties in the way of concluding the marriage. Go and have a drink and then we can talk.

HERR MAYER: It will pass, it will pass.

SEBASTIAN: I was promised 20,000 marks in dowry...

HERR MAYER: Water, I'm dying!

SEBASTIAN: I now hear from your daughter that you do not have this money.

HERR MAYER: It is the melancholy truth.

SEBASTIAN: Then I suggest you have a drink before we talk.

HERR MAYER: It can wait. Let us finish this conversation.

SEBASTIAN: You wish to marry your daughter off without a dowry? But what about our contract?

HERR MAYER: If you don't want her let her be.

SEBASTIAN: You promise me the dowry, and now you go back on your word.

HERR MAYER: Let us go.

SEBASTIAN: I can hardly believe such a thing.

HERR MAYER: Where are you going? There is the door.

SEBASTIAN: Am I to abandon her then?

HERR MAYER: As you please.

SEBASTIAN: I must either lose a girl I love, or see the ruin of my family.

HERR MAYER: Have you finished wearing out the carpets?

SEBASTIAN: Yes. I must sit down for a moment.

HERR MAYER: No!

SEBASTIAN: No, rather not.

HERR MAYER: Thank God for that.

SEBASTIAN: I shall talk to Florindo.

HERR MAYER: Yes, indeed.

SEBASTIAN: Something must be decided.

HERR MAYER: Yes, indeed.

SEBASTIAN: And you can go to Hell.

HERR MAYER: No, indeed.

SEBASTIAN: Oh, yes indeed, and we shall find out how poor you really are. (*Exit.*)

HERR MAYER: I am destitute. I have no safe. Has he gone? Farewell chest, farewell, my dear. I shall be back soon. I leave my heart behind with you. (*Exit.*)

CLARA: (*Entering.*) Can Florindo be amusing himself with me? At the same time as he is setting up his marriage to Stella? But why tell me he is leaving, when he would have to stay here with his bride? It still seems impossible. I suspect Sebastian invented such a fable because he had conceived some suspicion about Florindo and myself, and wished to discover my feelings. But if Florindo confirmed that he loved Stella, and in Sebastian's presence? Pah! He would say anything to support his friend. But if he had had any love for me, could he cause me such a torment? I do not know what to think.

TRIVELLINO: (*Enters.*) A visit.

CLARA: From whom?

TRIVELLINO: The Signora Stella.

CLARA: Better late than never.

TRIVELLINO: Do you mean that?

CLARA: Never mind.

TRIVELLINO: When she's gone, I've something to tell you.

CLARA: What?

TRIVELLINO: Later.

CLARA: Now.

TRIVELLINO: The Signora Stella is waiting.

CLARA: Let her.

TRIVELLINO: I know where your father's gold is.

CLARA: Where?

TRIVELLINO: Under his chair.

STELLA: (*Off.*) Clara, are you at home?

TRIVELLINO: I must dash.

CLARA: Was there a lot of gold?

TRIVELLINO: Masses.

CLARA: How did you get to see it?

TRIVELLINO: You see, you're worse than I am for nosiness.

STELLA: (*Enters, as TRIVELLINO leaves.*) *Liebchen*, pity me.

CLARA: I'm sorry to have kept you waiting. I was only half-dressed.

STELLA: Come, come, a little fib does no harm. I have been known to tell one myself from time to time.

CLARA: Why should you accuse me of lying?

STELLA: I could see you through the door.

CLARA: I wanted to see if you were over-curious.

STELLA: I have no wish to reply to that. I do not wish to become heated. We are friends, and shortly to be relations, so I have come to make you party to my prospects, immediate and glittering.

CLARA: Indeed. I should be glad to hear them.

STELLA: Has my brother said nothing to you?

CLARA: Should he have?

STELLA: Has he told you I am engaged to be married?

CLARA: Ah, yes... something of the sort.

STELLA: Good, then I can tell you Florindo has at last declared himself.

CLARA: I am delighted.

STELLA: Believe me, no more than I am.

CLARA: I do believe you. But does Signor Florindo really love you?

STELLA: Does he love me?

CLARA: I asked you first.

STELLA: Adores me. Poor boy. He suffered a whole month. Finally he was unable to contain himself any longer.

CLARA: He could not have done less than fall in love with you.

STELLA: I should consider I had lost my touch, if I could not make a man fall in love with me inside a month.

CLARA: What did you do to make him fall in love with you?

STELLA: What did you do to make my brother fall in love with you?

CLARA: Your brother fell in love with 20,000 marks.

STELLA: I should die of shame, if someone wished to marry me for my money.

CLARA: It would presuppose that you had some money to be married for, *nicht wahr*?

STELLA: Although I do not have a dowry, I have had more than enough proposals.

CLARA: But you have concluded none of them.

STELLA: Yes: this one.

CLARA: Concluded?

STELLA: It will be. Since we are friends, I know you wish me well, but there is just the faintest scintilla of envy, is there not?

CLARA: True. I envy your good qualities.

STELLA: No, but my good fortune.

TRIVELLINO: (*Enters.*) Signora, another visit.

CLARA: Who is it now, for goodness sake?

TRIVELLINO: The Signor Florindo.

STELLA: You see? He knew I was here, and he just could not keep himself from coming to see me.

CLARA: Could he not do that in your apartment? Whom did he ask for?

TRIVELLINO: For you, Signora.

STELLA: It is only polite to ask for the lady of the house.

CLARA: Does he know the Signora Stella is here?

TRIVELLINO: Not from me.

STELLA: Oh, he would know, he would know. He dogs me all the time.

CLARA: How nice.

TRIVELLINO: Shall I show him up?

STELLA: Yes, yes, have him up.

TRIVELLINO: Signora?

CLARA: Yes, yes, as you command. (*TRIVELLINO goes.*)

STELLA: Florindo has to go to Venice on business, and wants to hurry on the wedding. So, *Liebchen*, I expect I shall be married before you.

CLARA: How nice.

STELLA: Shall you come to my wedding?

CLARA: Of course. Of course. I shall be there.

STELLA: She said with some bitterness.

CLARA: We brides just can't have things sweet enough, can we?

STELLA: We? Oh, here he is, here he is. Isn't he handsome? Come in, come in, Signor Florindo. (*He does so.*) Don't be shy.

CLARA: What is this, Signor? Does my presence inhibit you from paying the necessary compliments to your bride-to-be? I shall withdraw.

FLORINDO: No, listen...

CLARA: To what, pray? To the sweet nothings you will whisper to her? Hardly suitable for a young girl's ears, would you say? If impatience to see her again has drawn you here, I do not need to be a party to your amorous intrigues...

FLORINDO: You cannot imagine...

CLARA: Oh, but I can, and with some ease. There is your bride-to-be: help yourself – to anything, you want.

FLORINDO: If you would stay...

CLARA: I marvel at you. You should know your duty better than to be so lukewarm, or perhaps lukecool. (*Exit.*)

STELLA: You hear? Eaten up with envy. She cannot bear to think of anyone being a bride but her. Well, now we are finally alone, dearest Signor Florindo, allow me to express my infinite satisfaction at the news relayed to me by my brother.

FLORINDO: What has he said to you?

STELLA: That you love me, and do me the honour of asking for my hand. When would you think of celebrating the wedding?

FLORINDO: We can conclude matters on my return from Venice.

STELLA: No, no, a thousand times no. I shall not trust in you in Venice alone.

FLORINDO: I have to go on business.

STELLA: I shall not prevent you from attending to it.

FLORINDO: I must go to Venice myself before bringing a
　　wife there.

STELLA: Then let us be married first: and go there after.

FLORINDO: Signora Stella... I would not wish to deceive
　　you. Once we are married, I fear you may regret it: I am
　　resolved to tell you the whole truth, while you are still free.

STELLA: Nothing can astonish me.

FLORINDO: Like most of my countrymen, I am very
　　jealous by nature, moody at the least thing.

STELLA: If you are jealous of me, it will be a sign of love.
　　I shall give you no cause to be jealous, and I shall suffer
　　if you are jealous without cause.

FLORINDO: Let us not speak of jealousy then. You will
　　hardly be in a position to make me so.

STELLA: Am I as unattractive as that?

FLORINDO: I did not say that. But I have my quirks. I do
　　not wish you to leave the house.

STELLA: I shall stay at home.

FLORINDO: Nor do I like you to receive visitors in the
　　house.

STELLA: It will be enough for me, if you are there.

FLORINDO: But shall I be? I like to amuse myself. I go
　　for walks.

STELLA: Quite right. A young man.

FLORINDO: Walks from which I often do not come home.

STELLA: When you have a wife, perhaps...

FLORINDO: You know so little of me. I gamble.

STELLA: With your own money.

FLORINDO: And sometimes frequent taverns with my
　　friends.

STELLA: Sometimes is all right.

FLORINDO: Since we are being candid, I must admit
　　I enjoy the company of women.

STELLA: Ah, as to that...

FLORINDO: You see? It might be better to forget all about
　　it. I am a dangerous fellow, a woman cannot suffer that
　　sort of thing. I am sorry, and sorry for you, and give you
　　back your freedom.

STELLA: Go and enjoy yourself, provided it is consonant
with your station.

FLORINDO: I don't know about that, and would not wish
to bind myself.

STELLA: Listen to me. If you behave badly, and if you
meet with some disgrace, the blame will be all your own.
I would not refuse you for that, and I would not cease to
love you for it – whatever happens.

FLORINDO: Only hear the rest.

STELLA: Tell me.

FLORINDO: I have a vicious temper.

STELLA: We all have our faults.

FLORINDO: If my brutality should ever make me lose
respect to you, if a blow should escape me...

STELLA: Offered to a woman of quality? Come, now.

FLORINDO: You are right, it would be an outrage. But
when I am in my rages I cannot contain myself. We must
dissolve this contract. You must have your freedom.

STELLA: Undo everything? Freedom? Beat me: murder me
if you will, I only wish to be yours.

FLORINDO: Mine?

STELLA: Yours. Indeed. Yes.

FLORINDO: With all these faults?

STELLA: When are we to be married?

FLORINDO: How can you love a man as wicked as I?

STELLA: If you were really wicked, you would hardly
advertise yourself in this way. Wicked men are wicked
because they do not consider themselves to be so.
Whoever knows himself, either is not wicked, or, if he is,
he may easily correct it. Your sincerity persuades me to
love you all the more – since, if you really lead a wicked
life, you will at least have warned me in good time: and
if not, my happiness will be all the greater. One way or
another, good or bad, you are mine, and I am yours,
despite all who may not wish it. Let us return to our
apartment, accompany me if you would not mind.

FLORINDO: Forgive me – just at the moment...

STELLA: Then I shall not leave until you are ready. I shall
keep Clara company for a space. (*Exit.*)

FLORINDO: (*Alone.*) Wonderful, wonderful, wonderful! In disentangling myself I end in worse toils than ever. But Stella is an extraordinary character; ready to suffer all, acquiescent, humble, patient, resigned; it should be easy to love a woman with such undeniable merits. In fact, during the month I have lived in their home I have always admired her conduct. All the more to be admired, that she never said anything until the day I was going to leave. She is good, wise, modest, beautiful... but not for me.

SEBASTIAN: (*Enters.*) Friend, when you finally decide to leave for Venice, we shall go together.

FLORINDO: (This threatens to become a party.) You wish to go to Venice too?

SEBASTIAN: Yes, I shall be company for you. I have talked to the old skinflint: he insists he has no money, and cannot give Clara a dowry. I love her, but I cannot allow myself to ruin her family: so it is necessary for me to detach myself. I have decided to go on my travels, and come with you.

FLORINDO: Are you abandoning Clara?

SEBASTIAN: If you put it like that. But what would you have me do? Marry her and ruin myself?

FLORINDO: I can hardly advise you to do that: but how can you have the heart to desert that girl?

SEBASTIAN: I know I shall regret it all my life. But what can a man of honour do? A wife costs a great deal, and if there should be children...

FLORINDO: But what will *she* do?

SEBASTIAN: Stay here, wretchedly looking after that avaricious old man. Or worse... in order to marry her off without a dowry, might he not pitch on some low fellow for her?

FLORINDO: How appalling.

SEBASTIAN: Perhaps some one who gambles, drinks, womanises, who might even beat her?

FLORINDO: Poor girl.

SEBASTIAN: She could be reduced to starvation.

FLORINDO: A girl of her beauty?

SEBASTIAN: I know all this, but I must leave her.

FLORINDO: Then you are decided? You are leaving her? To fall into the hands of Heaven knows who? Could you bear to see her married to someone else?

SEBASTIAN: If I cannot have her myself... I confess I should mind less if I could see her well married.

FLORINDO: Would you not be jealous?

SEBASTIAN: I should hardly have occasion to be so.

FLORINDO: Would you feel no grief?

SEBASTIAN: Love gives way to other feelings in time.

FLORINDO: If a friend of yours were to marry her?

SEBASTIAN: A friend? I don't understand.

FLORINDO: If... I don't know... for example... a name at random... myself.

SEBASTIAN: You can't marry her.

FLORINDO: Why not?

SEBASTIAN: You are engaged to my sister.

FLORINDO: No, but if... for example... for example... I were not?

SEBASTIAN: But even if you have not promised her, you have promised me.

FLORINDO: I know it seems like that. But if there had been, say... a misunderstanding?

SEBASTIAN: Now, how could there have been a misunderstanding? Your letter was quite manifestly clear.

FLORINDO: Yes, but... for example... if the letter had not been written to Stella?

SEBASTIAN: No, but... for example... who on earth else could it possibly have been written to?

FLORINDO: It could possibly have been written... for example... this is all in the realms of theory, of course... to Signora Clara.

SEBASTIAN: Hahahaha! What? You Clara's lover? Your best friend's rival? Dear friend, you have been reading too many novels and we must ration your visits to the theatre. You commit such an action, contrary to all laws of friendship? Ah, so that is why Clara has lost interest in me of late.

FLORINDO: Sebastian, do you still have that letter?

SEBASTIAN: Yes, somewhere, here.

FLORINDO: Read it again.

SEBASTIAN: Are you telling me you wrote it to Clara?

FLORINDO: Yes. I wrote it to her. You see what I wrote. That I was leaving, that I love her, that I know she loves me, but that I was leaving because I was honourable enough not to betray the laws of hospitality. Had I had time to finish it, I should have said that we could not go on with an affair of that sort, and that she should no longer reckon with me in this world. Sebastian, can you call that offence? Have I failed in duty, in friendship? I am in love with her, it is true: but it is you who are the cause. You introduced me, you gave me freedom, you gave me occasion. Had I been a man of a different character, I could have taken advantage of that freedom to satisfy my passion, but I have waited to declare it until I understood you had decided to abandon her, that taking her as a wife might be your financial ruin, and that she might fall into the hands of... unworthy people. If this is underhand behaviour, correct me... I am sorry, I withdraw, I ask your pardon.

SEBASTIAN: To see her married to you will be the greatest comfort I could wish in my trouble.

FLORINDO: Our friendship does not make things easier.

SEBASTIAN: I cannot have her. She must belong to you or to someone else.

FLORINDO: If that is how things are...

SEBASTIAN: Yes, that is just how things are. Marry her.

FLORINDO: What will Stella say?

SEBASTIAN: I shudder to think. But she will have flattered herself into a misunderstanding.

FLORINDO: Sebastian, I promise you will never regret this.

SEBASTIAN: I am no longer in a position to do so.

FLORINDO: I value your friendship more than anything in the world: I would let my love go for it, my life if need be.

SEBASTIAN: The more friend you are, the more willingly I see you married to her. (*Enter HERR MAYER.*)

HERR MAYER: *Meine Herren*, what are you doing here at this hour? Are you aware it is two o'clock in the morning? The lights are burning uselessly: I do not have money to throw away in this reckless fashion.

SEBASTIAN: Sir, we have something to discuss with you, which I hope will give you great pleasure.

HERR MAYER: I've finished with pleasure. Nothing gives it me any more.

SEBASTIAN: The matter could be profitable.

HERR MAYER: Pray Heaven it be so. Heaven knows I need it. Wait. Let me put out some of these candles. This light is dazzling me.

SEBASTIAN: I have to speak about your daughter, sir.

HERR MAYER: Speak about her all you want, just don't speak about a dowry.

SEBASTIAN: As you know, I am not in a position to take her without one.

HERR MAYER: Because you are a miser. A fortune hunter, I shouldn't wonder.

SEBASTIAN: If you say so – but from the love I still feel for Clara, I am proposing a happy opportunity to marry her without a dowry.

HERR MAYER: Did I hear you correctly?

SEBASTIAN: If you can ask such a question, it must mean you did.

HERR MAYER: At last: a man who can see the true worth of my daughter. Who is this estimable fellow?

SEBASTIAN: Here he is. The Signor Florindo. He has no need of the dowry. He is an only son, a rich man, he desires her for his wife. I yield my claim.

HERR MAYER: Oh, my dear, my very dear sir. Signor Florindo. Bless me. Would you take her without a dowry?

FLORINDO: Certainly, Signore; I love the girl and that will always be enough for me.

HERR MAYER: I can give her nothing, you know.

FLORINDO: No matter.

HERR MAYER: You will have to bear all the expenses.

FLORINDO: And shall.

HERR MAYER: Let me tell you something, in confidence.
Those few old rags she is wearing, I had them on credit,
and I really have no idea how I am to pay for them.
I shall have to... Tell me, would you have any difficulty
providing a little jointure, a counter-dowry?

FLORINDO: We can discuss the possibility.

HERR MAYER: Herr Sebastian, do something for me, run
up and call my daughter. In the meantime Signor
Florindo and I will put a few things down in writing.

FLORINDO: Shall you be giving her the news?

SEBASTIAN: With difficulty, but yes I shall. (*Exit.*)

HERR MAYER: Come now, Signore, the contract, the
contract. (*Producing a small scrap of paper.*) This will be big
enough. You see how things always come in handy.

FLORINDO: We shall not be able to agree to much on that.

HERR MAYER: The contract will either be very simple, or
I shall write very small. "The Signor Florindo degli
Ardenti promises to marry Fraulein Clara Mayer without
dowry, of any sort, without pretensions to, and renouncing
all claim or action to same, declaring himself neither to
need or desire same. Item: he promises to marry her
without wardrobe, without linen, with nothing, with
nothing, with nothing, taking and accepting her as she
was born. Item: he promises further to provide a
counter-dowry or jointure..." how much should we fix it at?

FLORINDO: I have no intention of providing a jointure.

HERR MAYER: Ah, now, without a jointure we can go no
further.

FLORINDO: How much do you propose?

HERR MAYER: 20,000 marks... to start with.

FLORINDO: Signor, that is too much.

HERR MAYER: I am getting the feeling you are a miser,
like the last one.

FLORINDO: That is correct, sir, I am a miser. Mean.

HERR MAYER: I have no wish to marry my daughter to a
miser.

FLORINDO: You would surely do well to do so, since she
is the daughter of a generous man.

HERR MAYER: Ah, if I had it, you would see just how
  generous. But in my present impoverished state... I once,
  when I was a young man, gave a dinner party for four
  friends. Cost me seven marks, for one dinner.

FLORINDO: Apiece?

HERR MAYER: Hardly.

FLORINDO: Good grief. Wasn't that rather overdoing things?

HERR MAYER: If I had those seven marks today, I should
  die a happy man.

FLORINDO: After all these years, you still mourn the loss
  of those seven marks?

HERR MAYER: And shall do for the rest of my life. But let
  us conclude matters. How much do you wish to give her
  in counter-dowry?

FLORINDO: Very well, let her have the 20,000 marks.

HERR MAYER: "... to give a counter-dowry or jointure of
  20,000 marks, payable on signature as herein stipulated
  to Herr Sigismund Mayer, father of the said..."

FLORINDO: Why to you?

HERR MAYER: The father is the legal administrator of his
  children's goods.

FLORINDO: And the husband is the legal administrator of
  his wife's goods. There will be no jointure except in the
  case of separation or death.

HERR MAYER: But, Signore, I must live on my daughter's
  jointure.

FLORINDO: Why?

HERR MAYER: Because I am a poor man.

FLORINDO: If you wish to come to Venice, I am yours to
  command.

HERR MAYER: I don't know how I shall live. Send some
  shirts for her, or she won't be able to leave the house.
  Just send the material, I can have the servants make
  them up. (And half a dozen for me at the same time.)

FLORINDO: Very well. And, if you permit, I shall send
  something so we can dine together.

HERR MAYER: Just give it to me, give it to me,
  I shall provide everything. You will see what fine

eggs, what excellent value for vegetables, what splendid capons. It will be a veritable feast. (*Exit.*)

SEBASTIAN: (*Coming back with CLARA.*) Signor Florindo, your bride.

FLORINDO: Sebastian, you are still feeling pain. There is still time. Where are you going?

SEBASTIAN: To undeceive my sister.

FLORINDO: Poor Stella.

SEBASTIAN: This is clearly a game of Unhappy Families, and my sister and I hold a winning hand. (*Exit.*)

FLORINDO: How can I let you continue in this unhappiness?

CLARA: Signor Florindo, it still seems to me you are more in love with your friend than with me.

FLORINDO: Cara Signora, my friend also has a claim on my heart.

CLARA: He cannot take me without a dowry. If you also abandon me, I know not what I shall do.

FLORINDO: That is what gives me the courage to marry you. Love must repair all the damage done to friendship.

HERR MAYER: (*Re-entering.*) Come, come, let us sign. Time is passing, the candles are being used up.

CLARA: I see there are difficulties for you.

FLORINDO: *Eccomi.* Let us sign immediately.

TRIVELLINO: (*Enters.*) *Mein Herr?*

HERR MAYER: What is it?

TRIVELLINO: A terrible thing.

HERR MAYER: What are you saying, wretched boy?

TRIVELLINO: Your treasure chest...

HERR MAYER: What are you rambling about? I have no treasure chest.

TRIVELLINO: No?

HERR MAYER: No.

TRIVELLINO: Oh, well, in that case, I shan't say another word.

HERR MAYER: Quickly, tell me, what's happened?

TRIVELLINO: The cookboy found a passage behind the wallpaper leading to your room.

HERR MAYER: My room?

TRIVELLINO: He opened the door from the inside.

HERR MAYER: Of my room?

TRIVELLINO: Yes, and dragged out a chest...

HERR MAYER: Ach, ach, ach.

TRIVELLINO: But if you haven't got a chest...

HERR MAYER: Mind your own business. I am a dead man. Where did he go? Where is he?

TRIVELLINO: He opened it up with a crowbar.

HERR MAYER: Oh, my poor darling. And then? And then?

TRIVELLINO: I don't know.

HERR MAYER: Quickly... at once... help... come with me. No, I don't want anybody. They will rob me... that damned boy... my poor darling... (*Exit.*)

CLARA: I must go with him. Come.

FLORINDO: I shall wait here.

CLARA: No, come with me.

FLORINDO: I beg you to excuse me.

CLARA: Of the two lovers who besiege me, I really don't know which to congratulate myself on more. (*Exit.*)

FLORINDO: Trivellino, what is this business? Has the chest been found?

TRIVELLINO: I knew it was there all the time. There's two of them, one for silver, one for gold.

FLORINDO: Did the Signora Clara know about them?

TRIVELLINO: Certainly. I told her.

FLORINDO: And she pretended to be in poverty.

TRIVELLINO: Of course.

FLORINDO: But why? Why?

TRIVELLINO: To avoid being married to Herr Sebastian.

FLORINDO: Could it have been?

TRIVELLINO: Of course it was. If you could see how much gold there is...

FLORINDO: Have you seen it?

TRIVELLINO: Of course.

FLORINDO: Run along and see if they need anything.

TRIVELLINO: Just looking at all that gold puts me in a good mood. (*Exit.*)

FLORINDO: This changes everything. Sebastian yielded her to me because of her poverty – and his. Now she is rich, the old man cannot deny her a dowry. If I marry her, I am in a way to commit larceny, and commit it on the dearest friend I have. What am I to do? What's this? Do you have to think about it? Sebastian must marry her, have the dowry, regain his love, and remedy the disorders of his household. But how to repair what has already been ill done? Tcha, the contract with her father has not been signed: it can be torn up. But what are Clara's feelings? That is the major difficulty. With the business so nearly concluded, it will be hard to calm her down. She must realise two things: first, where her duty lies, second, that she will never have me for a husband. For one, we need words, for the other, deeds.

STELLA: (*Entering.*) Signor Florindo?

FLORINDO: How may I serve you?

STELLA: Here. (*Holds out a knife to him.*)

FLORINDO: That is a paper-knife.

STELLA: Use it.

FLORINDO: What for?

STELLA: To kill me.

FLORINDO: Whyever?

STELLA: Because I have discovered you are to marry Clara.

FLORINDO: And for that you wish to die? So terrible a death. By paper-knife?

STELLA: Yes, if you wish to free yourself from a woman who will otherwise torment you for the rest of your life.

FLORINDO: Even in Venice?

STELLA: Anywhere in the baptised world. No, go among savages, I should follow you. Pursue you to the land of the aboriginals. If you knew how much I loved you, you would take pity on me.

FLORINDO: Do you not take it amiss, that I should have allowed a misunderstanding to circulate, to let it be understood I wanted to marry you to hide my love for someone else?

STELLA: You will not understand, will you? Nothing you do offends me: nothing you do displeases me. If you love me, I forget everything. If you do not, well... give it time. (*Re-enter SEBASTIAN.*)

SEBASTIAN: I congratulate you. I have seen the famous, the mysterious strongbox: there is a great deal of gold. The police have the matter in hand. A backstairs business. Clara will be rich. You will enjoy a considerable fortune.

STELLA: What has Signor Florindo to do with Clara?

FLORINDO: Sebastian, do you know me so little? Did you think I could do that to you? No. Clara is rich and Clara is yours. So you will not think I pretend, or believe that I might regret it, to give you assurance of my love, in your presence, I really do offer my hand in marriage to your sister, if she will still have me.

STELLA: If she will have you? Rest assured she will.

SEBASTIAN: I don't know what to say. I have always loved Clara, and the news that she will be able to make, or, at the very least, repair our family fortunes does nothing to diminish her attractions, I confess. But I yielded her to you: I cannot go back on that. I know what you would be sacrificing.

STELLA: Are you thinking of impeding him, brother?

SEBASTIAN: I shall not allow you to give your hand to my sister. Not for a whim, a scruple of honour.

STELLA: I am thunderstruck. He is marrying me because he loves me.

FLORINDO: It is true. I have finally recognised Signora Stella's good qualities.

SEBASTIAN: She may have good qualities and to spare, but I am quite sure you do not love her.

STELLA: We are turned mind-reader, I see. A fine support you are, brother.

SEBASTIAN: Forgive me, sister, and disabuse yourself. He is in love with Clara. The letter was to her, not you.

STELLA: He is talking in his sleep.

SEBASTIAN: Tell her the truth.

FLORINDO: It is true, Signora, I am ashamed to confess.

STELLA: Then you were just making fun of me?

FLORINDO: I ask forgiveness.

STELLA: You told me you were merely wicked, now I find you far worse; a bad-tempered, gambling, drunken, dissolute impostor. Get along, you are not worthy of me, and I shall shift well enough to do without you. (*Exit.*)

FLORINDO: Why did you stop me?

SEBASTIAN: The old man can no longer conceal the fact he is rich, he cannot deny Clara a dowry. She will be a rich bride, a catch, a considerable *partie*. I could not let you, by sacrificing love to friendship...

FLORINDO: ... do you the justice you deserve.

SEBASTIAN: But how can I hope that Clara... in love with you...

FLORINDO: Leave that to me.

SEBASTIAN: I am in your hands.

FLORINDO: Be in no doubt about that. (*As TRIVELLINO re-enters.*) Well, how do matters stand?

TRIVELLINO: The cookboy took to his heels. The police are after him now. I saw a lot of gold coins scattered on the floor. The old man came in and dragged the chest back into his room by main force. What with rage and grief he nearly tipped over twice. He was frightened half to death of being followed, he was hugging the chest, kissing it, trying to cover it up, to hide it... listen. (*Exit.*)

CLARA: (*Coming back in.*) Signor Florindo, my father is dead.

FLORINDO: Friend... the better for you.

SEBASTIAN: Who has the keys of the safe? (*Exit.*)

CLARA: Poor unfortunate old man. It was as good as murder. I feel dashed to pieces.

FLORINDO: Signora Clara, you have my deepest sympathy. Will you allow me to make a short speech? In this world we manufacture our own destinies, and, for most of us, it is our vices that trip us up in the end. Your father's avarice was the cause of a servant's discovering the treasure and trying to steal it, and the robbery was the cause of his death. Perhaps Heaven, to punish him for his fault, used the fault itself to punish him. You see the money was of little use in the end. In the midst of life we are in death, and all we can do is try to live honestly, knowing how to control our passions. Heaven at this moment offers you a fine opportunity to act with discretion and virtue. Try to find grounds for consolation in seeing yourself in a comfortable situation, with the dowry proper to you, and the hand of your devoted bridegroom, your most faithful Sebastian.

CLARA: Sebastian faithful, who abandoned me?

FLORINDO: Surely you can forgive a lover a jealous stratagem to test your heart?

CLARA: If he has gone about to test my heart, he will have discovered which way it is inclined. He has yielded me to you, and I am yours.

FLORINDO: Signora, you cannot be mine, if I cannot be yours.

CLARA: And why cannot you be mine?

FLORINDO: Because I am already married, to the Signora Stella.

CLARA: Married?

FLORINDO: That is so.

CLARA: When?

FLORINDO: I was ready to marry you when Sebastian was unable to do so. His love for you (and he is so worthy of yours) induced me to... sacrifice myself.

CLARA: Why?

FLORINDO: You deserve love... the regard I have for your qualities... what is the use of going on? From honour, gratitude, duty, all these, I have married Stella. It is superfluous to continue to expect anything more from me. You will say, how could I change from one moment to the next. My answer is I am not changeable. Nor was I trifling with you. Circumstances alter cases, and I must alter with them. When you were poor, Sebastian could not marry you, not from lack of love, but from cruel necessity. I took you...

CLARA: Out of pity.

FLORINDO: Out of love. But now you are rich, return to your first engagement. I have done what I must, and so must you. Learn from me how to conquer and suppress passion. Clara, I have loved you very much indeed, but for honesty and friendship, I have offered up my love on the altar of honour. I have married someone who is deserving of a husband's love, and in time I doubt not but that I shall come to recognise her qualities and my duties. Make up your mind to marry Sebastian. Let us both shut the doors on our past weaknesses, and see that an act of justice wipes out the memories of our loves, to render more final and complete the triumph of what we both know is right.

CLARA: Alas! What with my father's death and your unexpected words, I hardly know what world I am in.

FLORINDO: Behave with discretion and all will be well.

CLARA: You are cruel. What am I to do without a single friend to help and advise me?

FLORINDO: There is Sebastian.

CLARA: He will despise me.

SEBASTIAN: (*Re-entering.*) No, my dearest, I have no reason to do that. I am yours, if you will have me.

CLARA: Must I marry the moment my father dies?

FLORINDO: Give your promise, confirm it, and the rest can be done all in good time.

CLARA: Oh, heavens!

SEBASTIAN: Come, in token of love and fidelity, give me your hand.

CLARA: Enough, Signore. I reproach nothing but my own weakness. I say now, in front of Sebastian, I have had a regard for you, though you have never, never deserved it.

FLORINDO: Signora, you mortify me with good reasons. Still, it seems to me, despite your disdain, you have some tenderness left for me.

CLARA: Your vanity is leading you astray. To undeceive you as effectively as possible, you see me ready to give my hand to my husband.

SEBASTIAN: Clara, angel!

CLARA: I have not yet said it was you.

SEBASTIAN: Who then, my dearest?

FLORINDO: Heavens! Face the truth, do not flatter yourself with hopes of me.

CLARA: No! I do not. I admire you, Signor Florindo, I admire you, and I do not condemn you. I hope my marriage will be happy, since it will be the work of a virtuous heart. You teach me to subjugate the passions, and I promise to triumph over them by your example. Sebastian will have no reason to complain of me. Sebastian! Here is my hand. Yes, here it is, as Signor Florindo instructs me. If he has not loved me, I must not be sorry to give him up. If he *has* loved me, and is giving me up for whatever reason, I must show myself no less strong than he. In any event, Sebastian, I shall be your wife. Here is my hand. With it you gain control over my inheritance: with discretion and prudence, you may gain control over my heart – in time.

SEBASTIAN: I hope to make myself worthy of it. (For the moment, control over the money is no small gain.)

FLORINDO: Heaven be praised, here is an affair concluded which has cost me much pain, and is like to go on doing so for some time to come. Heaven bless you both. I shall leave for Venice at once.

CLARA: Contented, with your admirable bride.

FLORINDO: Ah, Signora, do not be deceived...

CLARA: Write every day, for the love of Heaven. If you don't feel the need to, write just one line: "Today, such and such a date, I don't want to write to you..." For Heaven's sake, don't fabricate your letters, and never, *never* reread them. You see, I am tempted to shine in front of you. Did you think I was exempt from the sin of vanity? But I want to shine by honesty alone.

FLORINDO: Signora, I may have known cleverer women than you, but none more honest.

CLARA: I have such a wish to love you I even show you the way to oblige me to do so.

STELLA: (*Entering.*) I congratulate you.

CLARA: And I you.

STELLA: I am being married out of pity.

CLARA: And I am taking a husband out of necessity.

FLORINDO: Signora Stella, let us be off for Venice at once. The fine moral lesson I have read Signora Clara could easily be undone for the very reasons which made

it so necessary in the first place. Wife, this heart is yours.
But allow me, if you will, to leave a piece of it behind
with these two good people, and go away, wearing in its
place an honourable scar to let the world know the duties
of a constant friend.

(*SEBASTIAN, FLORINDO and STELLA leave. CLARA is alone.
Enter TRIVELLINO.*)

TRIVELLINO: Dinner is served, signorina.

(*A long pause, while CLARA is immobile.*)

Signorina?

(*CLARA raises her head at last, and walks firmly out.
TRIVELLINO snuffs the candles before leaving.*)

THE BATTLEFIELD

La Guerra

(1760)

for
Gerard Murphy

CHARACTERS

EGIDIO,
commander of the besieged city

FLORIDA,
his daughter

SIGISMONDO,
general of the besieging army

CONTE,
lieutenant

CLAUDIO,
lieutenant

FERDINANDO,
ensign

FAUSTINO,
ensign

CIRILLO,
lieutenant, crippled

POLIDORO,
quartermaster to the army

ASPASIA,
his daughter

LISETTA,
a country girl

ORSOLINA,
market woman selling to the army

FABIO,
ensign

ADJUTANT

CORPORAL

COURIER

Soldiers, citizens

This translation was first performed at the Citizens' Theatre Glasgow in August 1980, translated and directed by Robert David MacDonald, designed by Philip Prowse, with the following cast:

CONTE, Andrew Wilde

FAUSTINO, Ciaran Hinds

FLORIDA, Angela Chadfield

FERDINANDO, Robert Gwilym

ASPASIA, Di Trevis

CORPORAL, John Breck

POLIDORO, Roger McKern

CIRILLO, Gordon Hammersley

ORSOLINA, Ida Schuster

SOLDIER 1, Bill Leadbitter

SOLDIER 2, Mark Rylance

LISETTA, Sian Thomas

SIGISMONDO, Steven Dartnell

EGIDIO, Patrick Hannaway

FABIO, Dennis Knotts

COURIER, Mark Rylance

ENSEMBLE, Jo Buckle, Gerry Mcgrath, Ron Findlay, Gerry Mcmonagle, Michael Lancaster, Roderick Stewart, Alan Mcculloch

The production was presented at the Venice Biennale in 1981 with the following changes:

FAUSTINO, Gordon Hammersley

FLORIDA, Jill Spurrier

ASPASIA, Frances Barber

CIRILLO, Ciaran Hinds

ENSEMBLE, David Balfour, Trisha Biggar, Billy Jones, Colin MacNeil, Christina Thornton

Assistant Director, Kim Dambaek

ACT ONE

Officer's mess

The CONTE, FABIO and other OFFICERS playing cards. FLORIDA and FAUSTINO talking together. FERDINANDO and ASPASIA at another table, drinking. A CORPORAL in attendance.

CONTE: Two sevens.

FAUSTINO: Donna Florida, will you not permit me to try my fortune at the faro bank?

FLORIDA: I am as much distressed as amazed the desire for play should enter your head.

FAUSTINO: Amazed?

FLORIDA: It is nearly day. At any moment you could be ordered to the assault, and can you be so thoughtless of the danger, so unprepared, as to have the heart for play?

FAUSTINO: What more can I do? If I am called to the field, I must obey. I may be killed, but thinking of danger is no way to avoid it. Let me then enjoy these few moments of peace, and if it displeases you that I should play, give me at least the consolation of your smile.

CONTE: And another pair! Long live the Knave! Excellent pretty boy.

FERDINANDO: Conte, how fares the game?

CONTE: Excellent well, my dear: I shall now proceed, with the blessing of Heaven, to break the bank. Wait! Double or quits on the king.

FERDINANDO: Bravo!

CONTE: *Corraggio!*

FAUSTINO: Let me risk two zecchini.

FLORIDA: No, for the moment, I would not wish you to play.

FAUSTINO: You are the mistress to command.

CONTE: *Diavolo!*

FERDINANDO: How are things, Conte?

CONTE: Nothing, nothing. Shuffle, my dear: I shall return for my revenge. A glass of burgundy.

(*He goes over to ASPASIA's table.*)

FERDINANDO: Taste this: a gift from Madamigella Aspasia.

CONTE: *Che viva Madamigella*! (*Tasting.*) Word of a cavalier. Ah, but in the quartermaster's mess everything must be of the first quality. Happy the man who is in his daughter's good graces.

FERDINANDO: And what is that supposed to mean?

CONTE: Merely that...

FABIO: Conte, the cards are cut.

CONTE: *Eccomi.* (*Returns to the card table.*) Ten zecchini on the seven.

FAUSTINO: But Donna Florida, would you drive me to despair? This is perhaps the last time we shall be together. How can you still treat me with such want of charity?

FLORIDA: Oh, *cieli*, my father is commander of the very fortress you are besieging. At the approach of your armies, he made arrangements to remove me from danger. But, on the very eve of our departure, your armies surprised the suburbs, and, small merit to you, took me prisoner. Now I am held here these ten weeks, a hostage, perhaps to be used as a counter, no more, no less, for bargaining or blackmail. The destiny of arms is uncertain: and would you have me merry and uncaring?

FAUSTINO: I feel both for you and with you, but I cannot but be impatient. At least permit me to amuse myself at the table. Better I should bleed freely there than elsewhere.

FLORIDA: Can you still joke? Oh, go, go, ingrate, go in my despite.

FAUSTINO: No, *carina*, forgive me. I shall not talk of play again.

CONTE: The damned seven's gone. To the devil I hope.

ASPASIA: The Conte is losing, Ferdinando.

FERDINANDO: Let him: I hope to win a thousandfold.

CONTE: Upon what battlefield?

FERDINANDO: Your heart.

ASPASIA: You make me laugh.

FERDINANDO: That is depressingly clear.

ASPASIA: Have you no thought for the war?

FERDINANDO: A soldier is paid to obey not to think.
I leave that to the generals. It is only on the field the
danger lies, and one is as well two hundred yards away
from it as two hundred miles. Tomorrow I shall fight,
if I must; tonight, I shall amuse myself, if I can. Your
company delights me, you are amiable, you are
attractive, you are... Your health.

CONTE: Strumpet fortune! Am I condemned to perpetual
ill-luck? Everything on the seven.

FLORIDA: You see the poor Conte, how the game upsets
him: would you expose yourself to a like agitation?

FAUSTINO: Have you no feeling for me?

FLORIDA: The situation in which we find ourselves hardly
permits more.

CONTE: The third seven gone. Are they all against me?
I want to see the fourth. Twenty zecchini on the fourth
seven.

ASPASIA: Conte, I cannot allow you credit.

CONTE: My dear, you have the word of an officer and a
gentleman.

ASPASIA: Forgive me...

FABIO: You know we do not play on credit in the field.

CONTE: (*To FERDINANDO.*) Lend me twenty zecchini.

FERDINANDO: Did I but have it.

CONTE: Don Faustino, my dear, lend me twenty zecchini.

FAUSTINO: Word of a gentleman, I do not have it.

CONTE: Corporal.

CORPORAL: Word of a... Signore?

CONTE: Send for the quartermaster.

CORPORAL: Right away, signore.

FLORIDA: Corporal?

CORPORAL: Signora?

FLORIDA: What news from the camp?

CORPORAL: Our engineers have commenced a breach in
the enemy walls.

FLORIDA: *Povera me!* What shall become of my father?

CONTE: There goes the seven. And I couldn't play. Where
is that damned fool quartermaster, may he rot in hell?

ASPASIA: Can it be my father you speak of, Conte?

CONTE: Of course: excellent fellow, salt of the earth, always said so.

POLIDORO: (*Entering, with the CORPORAL.*) Who is asking for me?

CONTE: Signor Commissario, the very man: be good enough to let me have twenty zecchini.

POLIDORO: Twenty zecchini?

CONTE: Twenty zecchini.

POLIDORO: For whom?

CONTE: For me.

POLIDORO: To play?

CONTE: To play.

POLIDORO: Twenty zecchini?

CONTE: Twenty zecchini.

POLIDORO: *Benissimo.*

CONTE: Then stir yourself, damn you.

POLIDORO: A moment. (*Consulting a small notebook.*)

CONTE: Would you put me out of patience?

POLIDORO: A moment. (*Reading.*) "The signor Conte, lieutenant of horse, promises to pay on account of wages, the sum of sixty zecchini."

CONTE: And twenty makes eighty.

POLIDORO: *Con permesso*, a small matter.

CONTE: Namely?

POLIDORO: A guarantee.

CONTE: A guarantee? From a gentleman of my standing? I am not unknown in the army.

POLIDORO: *Benissimo.*

CONTE: *Benissimo, benissimo*, and you still demand a guarantee?

POLIDORO: It was not a financial guarantee I had in mind.

CONTE: What then?

POLIDORO: A guarantee that tomorrow morning a cannon ball will not crown the military career of the signor Conte, and send my twenty zecchini to join him in the Elysian Fields.

CONTE: In which case the affair will be settled.

POLIDORO: *Benissimo.*

CONTE: If not, I shall rest your debtor for one hundred zecchini. Does that satisfy you?

POLIDORO: I think on that risk, we might accommodate you.

CONTE: Then give them here.

POLIDORO: A moment.

(*He consults his notebook again.*)

CONTE: That wretched notebook will drive me mad. Wait for me, my dears, I'll be with you straight.

FABIO: We shall not stir.

POLIDORO: *In toto*: one hundred zecchini. Be good enough to sign here.

CONTE: *Benissimo.*

POLIDORO: You took the very word out of my mouth. Here you are.

CONTE: *Obligatissimo.* (*Goes back to the table.*) *Eccomi qui.* Cut the cards.

ASPASIA: *Serva sua*, father dear.

POLIDORO: Daughter, you here? What are you about?

ASPASIA: I was held here in conversation... conversation.

POLIDORO: *Benissimo.*

(*Exit.*)

ASPASIA: (*To FERDINANDO.*) My father is the dearest man in all the world.

FERDINANDO: There is only one question to which I want the answer *Benissimo.*

ASPASIA: Before you ask for his answer, perhaps you should be sure of mine.

FERDINANDO: And what would that be?

ASPASIA: If it is your intention to go to the barricades, depressing.

FERDINANDO: And if I return in one piece.

ASPASIA: *Benissimo.*

FERDINANDO: Then I have all my wish. Your health.

ASPASIA: (*To the CORPORAL.*) Bring another bottle.

FLORIDA: Donna Aspasia is amusing herself famously enough.

FAUSTINO: The gold that is poured into the mouth of war does not return to the earth in the usual way: it sticks to the hands of certain people, and quartermasters for certain.

CONTE: Three zecchini left. All on the seven.

FLORIDA: You hear? If the Conte loses that as well, I fear we may be witnesses to an unfortunate scene.

FAUSTINO: There are too many of us: he would never dare anything excessive.

CONTE: Oh, *indiavolato*, vile seven, *maledetissimo*! Give me those cards. (*Tears them.*) Devil take the man who printed them, the men who won them, and myself for losing with them!

ASPASIA: Now let us have no nonsense.

CONTE: Ehi, what matter. What's done is done. Think no more of it. Cheerly, my dears, cheerly. Give me something to drink. A good wine, a good fight, and a good fff... friend to enjoy it with, even if it's that damned ensign who has just ruined me, my dear.

FABIO: *Amico*, there is no railing at fortune.

CONTE: You are in the right of it. Come, give me a kiss, my dear: you are an honest fellow, and I have shown myself a nincompoop. Now I have no money left to play, I shall have to make desperate love to someone. Is there no room by either of these ladies?

ASPASIA: Come, come, *signor tenente*, think of your companions at the batteries, whither you may at any moment be sent to join them.

CONTE: Must we fight? Then let us fight. Mount the breach? Storm the walls? You see me a ready man. But while I stand here, I think not of it: I must amuse myself, make tyrannic love to you.

FLORIDA: Signor Conte, it is hardly for you to take such a liberty.

CONTE: Pish, tush, away with you, what business can you have with that boy? I shall be your cicerone through the delicious meanderings of life.

FAUSTINO: Conte, a little more respect to the lady, if you please.

CONTE: Respect? Respect? I hope I am not lacking in that quarter, my dear. If she is conversing with you, she is at liberty to do so. And then she can talk to me. (*He sits close to FLORIDA.*)

FLORIDA: That is an impertinence.

CONTE: Do not make my blood boil.

FAUSTINO: If it is over-heated, I shall be glad to let a little of it.

CONTE: I'll teach you how a gentleman handles a sword.

ASPASIA: Ehi, signori, in the quartermaster's mess?

CONTE: In the quartermaster's mess, indeed, where officers are fleeced, where the blood of the regiment is sucked dry, and where your worthy father, for the sake of twenty zecchini will be good enough to allow us to fight a duel.

FERDINANDO: *Caro amico,* this is neither the time nor the place. Should the General get wind...

CONTE: You are right. We shall fight after the battle, my dear.

FAUSTINO: Whenever you will.

FLORIDA: Oh, Heavens. Have you so little regard for life? I am no longer surprised you should wish to pass the hours before a battle in gaming. I thought your vaunted love of glory might have made you ambitious to win it under the eyes and orders of your General. I thought you might go with stoic indifference to a glorious victory or a hero's death. But when I see you risking an inglorious death, and in so wretched a cause, I can only think you are ruled by fanaticism rather than reason. Joking about death has made his name familiar to you, and you meet his blows from habit, not courage. You say you love glory: then value the life that would enable you to win it, above the vanity of unthinking vainglorious bravado. (*Exit.*)

CONTE: Such lectures, my dear, such tirades...

FAUSTINO: Donna Florida is speaking the truth.

CIRILLO: (*Hobbling in.*) *Allegri, compagni.* We have advanced into the breach: three and a half feet.

CONTE: How can you know? It isn't daylight yet.

CIRILLO: One can see clearly enough across the field. I aimed a brace of cannon. Spiked one of the enemy's field pieces. A shot, a shot, a perfect shot.

ASPASIA: Don Cirillo, are you not afraid a cannonade may take off your other leg?

CIRILLO: Legs? Legs? What use are legs to me? For the pleasure of spiking a cannon I would give ten legs, if I still had them. *Animo*, what are we about? Is there no play?

FABIO: There was till now.

CONTE: I lost my shirt – and cuffs.

CIRILLO: And Don Fabio?

CONTE: Has been winning.

CIRILLO: And Don Ferdinando?

CONTE: Has been drinking.

CIRILLO: Bravo, and Don Faustino?

CONTE: Has been making love.

CIRILLO: Bravissimo: time spent in reconnaissance is never wasted. *Amici*, in another two hours at the most, we shall be mounting the guard on their ramparts. The enemy is defending himself most desperately. They made a sortie, the very devil, we repulsed it, but it cost us thirty men: and the fire coming from the besieged garrison, you never saw anything like it. But you shall, you shall: till when let us amuse ourselves.

CONTE: Give me a drink.

FERDINANDO: Yes, indeed.

CIRILLO: Drink?

FAUSTINO: With pleasure.

FERDINANDO: With permission of the lady of the house.

ASPASIA: Make yourselves at home.

CIRILLO: Gentlemen, His Majesty!

TUTTI: The King!

ASPASIA: I don't know how they do it.

FERDINANDO: To our General.

ASPASIA: All this gaiety.

TUTTI: *Evviva*!

FAUSTINO: To the brave lads at the barricades.

TUTTI: *Evviva*!

ASPASIA: And in half an hour they'll be under fire.

CONTE: And long live us, by the way, who are about to face the foe.

TUTTI: *Evviva!*

CIRILLO: To the first man to mount the breach.

CONTE: With modesty, that shall be I.

FERDINANDO: Pardon me, Conte, I have precedence: my regiment is senior to yours.

CONTE: Then, my dear, I shall distinguish myself with the vanguard at the redoubt.

FERDINANDO: I shall not permit such interference.

CONTE: I hardly feel I must wait for your permission, my dear.

CIRILLO: Come, lads, to courage, anyway. Now let us amuse ourselves.

FERDINANDO: Madamigella, will you dance?

ASPASIA: Willingly.

CONTE: You dance, we'll drink.

(*CIRILLO plays the flute, FERDINANDO and ASPASIA dance.*)

FABIO: (*Entering.*) Gentlemen: the General has convened a council of war. The high command is already assembled in his tent, and he has requested all officers to hold themselves under orders.

FERDINANDO: What is the council about, do you know?

FABIO: They are deciding on the final assault. (*Drum.*) Let us go, gentlemen.

CONTE: Into the breach. (*Exit.*)

CIRILLO: Once more.

FERDINANDO: To the fray. (*Exit.*)

FAUSTINO: To glory? (*Exit.*)

CIRILLO: Hand me my crutch. (*Exit.*)

ASPASIA: Oh, get along with you, Don Cirillo, you are exempt from such exertions. Rest, rest, now. Take the weight off your feet... foot.

CIRILLO: Give me that crutch!

ASPASIA: I shall do no such thing. You have laid down your leg, now lay down your arms. (*Exit.*)

CIRILLO: *Maledettissima!* I wish to go to the breach, the barricade, the cannonade, and go to them I shall.

(*Exit, supporting himself on a chair.*)

Another part of the camp

POLIDORO: Pfui! A marvellous fine thing, war. I always speak well of it: no danger of a vote for peace from me. Some might say I was like the hangman's wife who prayed Heaven to increase her husband's business. But breathes there a soul alive does not desire his own advantage? Quarrels give bread to lawyers, illnesses to doctors, and where's the doctor or lawyer would have all men hale and all families at peace? Were there no wars, there would be no quartermasters, and who, in a way to put by 100,000 scudi in four, five years of war, would raise a little finger, much less his voice, to desire peace? Who exclaims against war? Those who have seen their country laid waste, not those who sell grain and wine at high prices to armies. Who bewails war? Merchants who suffer the damage of interrupted trade: not those who serve the needs of the armies at 20 or 30 per cent. Who weeps for the war? Those who lose a father, a son, a husband: not those who welcome them home laden with booty and honour. Who laments the war? Soldiers betimes, and officers too, when they find themselves in want: not quartermasters who swim in abundance, coining money from supply and demand, and filtering the gold and silver of an entire army into their own pockets.

ORSOLINA: (*Entering with her cart.*) *Serva, signor commissario.*

POLIDORO: Orsolina, what are you doing here? At this hour?

ORSOLINA: I came to give you an account of my winnings last night.

POLIDORO: *Benissimo.*

ORSOLINA: That's sixty bottles of Chianti sold, thirty of Burgundy, sixteen of Rosolino, twenty-two drums of brandy, forty screws of smoking tobacco, fifty-three of chewing, and a case of pipes.

POLIDORO: *Benissimo.*

ORSOLINA: So here's the capital back you were good enough to lend me, and for the profit, I rely on your generosity. As ever.

POLIDORO: How much?

ORSOLINA: *Dio mio*, as I am an honest woman, I made double on the wine, a third on the rosolino, and two thirds on the rest.

POLIDORO: *Benissimo.* Are you among those who speak ill of the war?

ORSOLINA: Me? I was a poor washerwoman. Came to the camp with my husband, as a follower. The war soon made me a widow, you soon helped me to a stall, and with my wit and your support, I hope to return home and live like a lady.

POLIDORO: *Benissimo.*

ORSOLINA: Don't you want the money?

POLIDORO: No, *gioia mia*, keep it, increase and multiply. You need more wine? I shall let you have it. I respect a woman who can make much of little. That is how I did things myself, and once the war is done, perish the day, if I should resolve to take a wife... enough said, I have an inclination for you.

ORSOLINA: Oh, *signor commissario*, can you think a poor laundress flatters herself she could become the wife of a quartermaster?

POLIDORO: Laundress? Pooh, you are a merchantwoman now. Money is the future: it sponges out the past. Who would believe what I was before I became a quartermaster? I was, in confidence, you understand, a poor drummer-boy. I rose to be shop-boy to a camp-follower: saved ten scudi: bought a donkey: traded with the army. Then I was in charge of the mules, went on to be warehouse man for the grain supplies, interested myself in the bakeries, made the jump to general purveyor, behaved with prudence, made myself agreeable to the staff officers, laid out money with good judgment and bribes with good timing, and here I am arrived at the Himalayas of war quartermastership. What do you say to that?

ORSOLINA: What you would say yourself. *Benissimo.*

POLIDORO: Money and money make the best match in the world.

ORSOLINA: But I shall never have any.

POLIDORO: Pish, make it. I respect a woman who makes a lira a day of her own, more than one who spends a scudo a day, of her husband's. Dividends fluctuate: hard work looks after itself.

ORSOLINA: Spoken like the man you are. I shall see any money you give me bears fruit. I thought to set up two or three faro banks in the shop, buy snuff boxes and watches off the gamblers against an advice at no risk, and a lightning profit, especially in wartime, mm?

POLIDORO: *Benissimo.* And may I advise, a little black book...

ORSOLINA: ... to render you accounts of every transaction I make.

POLIDORO: *Benissimo.*

ORSOLINA: And when the war is won, by whoever... (*She draws close to him.*)

POLIDORO: (*Evading her.*) I see two sergeants waiting for me. *Orsolina mia, a rivederci...*

ORSOLINA: Don't forget me now.

POLIDORO: Never fear.

ORSOLINA: I have an inclination for you as well.

POLIDORO: *Benissimo.*

ORSOLINA: You will have no cause to complain.

POLIDORO: *Benissimo.* (*Exit.*)

ORSOLINA: A fine stroke of luck for me, a chance to become a real damned lady at one go. Who knows? Oh, Heaven bless, preserve and keep the war going. Where else can you find these feverish fits of fortune? Here is the quartermaster's daughter: no bad thing if I were to get into her good graces: no sense having an enemy in the house.

ASPASIA: (*Entering.*) What are you doing here?

ORSOLINA: Looking for you, *illustrissima.*

ASPASIA: Well, my good woman, and what can I do for you?

ORSOLINA: I need your protection.

ASPASIA: Go on.

ORSOLINA: As you may know, I have a little stall. I make a small profit now and then: and for that I am robbed, envied, persecuted.

ASPASIA: Poor creature.

ORSOLINA: It is true the *signor commissario* has shown me a certain kindness, but I should be glad of the illustrious patronage of your good self.

ASPASIA: What do you sell?

ORSOLINA: A little of everything. Wine, brandy, tobacco are the mainstays of my trade: but I do a little in the way of haberdashery. This little work-box, look, isn't it pretty?

ASPASIA: Oh, very, yes.

ORSOLINA: English work.

ASPASIA: One can see. I dote on it.

ORSOLINA: Your ladyship has wonderful taste.

ASPASIA: I hardly ever saw a prettier. (If she wants my protection, she'd better give it to me)

ORSOLINA: (She's in love with it. I'll keep her on the hook.) See all the pretty fixings.

ASPASIA: It is the dearest thing. How dear, by the way?

ORSOLINA: To anyone who wanted it, it must be worth six zecchini.

ASPASIA: Six? Zecchini? Are you not ashamed? It is quite pretty, I grant, and I might have bought it – but six zecchini! I see now what you are afraid of. You buy goods, sell them at twice their value, and then have the impertinence to ask for my protection. Protect a cheat, a usurer? I shall have my father close your shop. I shall have you chased out of camp.

ORSOLINA: *Perdoni, illustrissima.* I said that to anyone who wanted it, it would be worth six zecchini: but I did not think then you would wish to buy it. If you want it, it is yours.

ASPASIA: How much?

ORSOLINA: The honour of your patronage is enough for me.

ASPASIA: Oh, but...

ORSOLINA: Listen, signora. In all sincerity, I sell it for six zecchini, but it cost me somewhat less. Take it as a gift, if you would deign to, and leave me the worry of making up the loss.

ASPASIA: Poor woman. I sympathise with you.

ORSOLINA: My feelings exactly. That is why I commend myself to your protection.

ASPASIA: Yes, yes, dear soul, have no fear.

ORSOLINA: And my regards to your father, dear, good, generous man that he is.

ASPASIA: And... if you lay your hand on anything pretty, let me see it... first.

ORSOLINA: Never fear. (Larceny in the blood.) (*Exit.*)

ASPASIA: I'm always kind when I can be. It makes you liked. That poor soul works hard, and one may see she has a good heart.

FLORIDA: (*Entering.*) Donna Aspasia, for pity's sake, support me.

ASPASIA: Donna Florida, what has chanced that I see you thus agitated?

FLORIDA: You know they are holding a council of war?

ASPASIA: They hold them all the time: I no longer have even the curiosity to ask what about.

FLORIDA: They are deciding the final fate of my country, perhaps even of my father's life.

ASPASIA: Would you rather we lost the battle and were cut to pieces?

FLORIDA: We? Oh, I no longer know who my enemy is. I long only for peace, not for the death of a living soul.

ASPASIA: *Cara*, your heart is only half in the fortress.

FLORIDA: You reprove me for loving Don Faustino? It is true. The uniform he wears should make me hate him: but his qualities breached all my defences. And now, oh God, the war rages fiercer than ever, the fortress is besieged, the breach is opened, and they talk of taking the citadel by storm. I tremble for the danger to my father: I confess, yes, I tremble for the danger of my lover. My heart fights more fiercely with itself than two opposing armies, and win or lose must be equally terrible for me.

ASPASIA: You are not bred to the war, and you are still susceptible to the littlest apprehension. For myself, more than a hundred officers, all desperate for my love, to hear

them talk, have been killed in battle. At first I was sorry
for a particular loss; now, after so many, I hear of the
death of such and such a one, as if they had told me he
had lost at cards. What else is war but a game of chance?
For all the strategy of the commanders, and the courage of
the commanded, death is chance. Guns do not think: they
hit or they miss. And they may miss the greatest coward,
just as they may hit the greatest hero. When I talk with the
officers who are to fight, I feel I am talking with shadows.
Shadows are all alike: therefore I treat them all alike: I let
them go without thinking. I rejoice with those who return,
I forget those who do not, I joke with the living, and do
not lament for the dead.

FLORIDA: I too am a soldier's daughter, but I do not have
your force of habit, nor the courage on which you pride
yourself, nor can I have it, and permit me to say, no girl
should have it: for all your heroic statements, nature
should rouse herself: love, reason, blood, work, and
every feeling counsel fear and pity.

ASPASIA: I wished only to divert your spirits: but here is
one who will surely succeed where I have failed.

FLORIDA: Who?

FAUSTINO: (*Entering.*) *Eccomi a voi, adorata donna Florida*!

FLORIDA: Is the council over?

FAUSTINO: Yes.

FLORIDA: What have they decided?

FAUSTINO: They are to give the assault to the fortress.
They will enter through the breach, and if the garrison
will not surrender, they will be made prisoners of war.

ASPASIA: Fine news for Donna Florida.

FLORIDA: Ah, cruel man, how can you bring such news
with such indifference?

FAUSTINO: Do not you too desire the termination of the
present campaign? In one day now, valour and the
fortunes of war will decide for or against us.

FLORIDA: Us? For or against my father.

FAUSTINO: Donna Florida, while we are in the field,
I must consider him my enemy. I would feel the same

were it my own father. An officer swears unconditional loyalty to his sovereign, and must prefer honour and victory to all other benefits of this life.

ASPASIA: You hear? With talk like that dinning in your ears all day long, can you wonder I have become a heroine perforce?

FLORIDA: Have you no feeling for what I am suffering? Or did you come on purpose to insult me?

FAUSTINO: I came to bid you farewell, perhaps for the last time.

FLORIDA: Ah, then you too fear we shall never meet again?

ASPASIA: Would you rather he did not? All passions seek whatever nourishes them, and fear loves the idea of danger. Love is a fine spur, but so is fear, and no man who is not afraid can be a hero. We would all be cowards if only we dared. *Cara*, the age of armour and chain mail is long past. He must go naked as you see him, or would like to see him, beneath a hail of grapeshot, to scale the walls, and they will rain down stones, lead, artillery and I know not what, and by God, signor ensign, if they hit you, there will not be a bone of you left to say a prayer over.

FLORIDA: Be still, for pity's sake. Have you the heart to laugh?

ASPASIA: Force of habit.

FAUSTINO: Donna Florida, in these last moments, do not send me away without a glance of compassion.

FLORIDA: Oh, go, Tartar, go, and if you should meet with my father, forget you ever knew I was his daughter.

FAUSTINO: Whatever my fate, I meet it with more indifference than I receive your dislike. Oh, Donna Florida, I swear if I survive to love you for ever and if it at all lie in my power, to make you happy.

ASPASIA: (Death at his elbow, and he still wants to make love.)

FAUSTINO: One loving word, and I shall go with more courage to the field. The mere fact that I speak at this moment of my love should assure you of its sincerity. One word.

CORPORAL: (*Entering.*) Signor Ensign, quickly. The regiment is under arms, and is awaiting the first signal for the assault.

FAUSTINO: Donna Florida, farewell. Permit me to consign to you my rings, my watch, my snuffbox, my purse: if I am to live, be you their trustee, if to die, dispose of them as you please. (*Drum.*) Love me, if I am worthy of it, and let hap what Heaven wills.
(*Exit with the CORPORAL.*)

FLORIDA: Stop him!

ASPASIA: Not a chance. A drum can deafen a soldier to all else.

FLORIDA: What are all these things?

ASPASIA: He left them for you to dispose of when he is killed.

FLORIDA: Ah, no, I feel enough grief without new objects to awaken it.

CORPORAL: (*Entering.*) Signore, the General commands me to inform you that prayers will be offered for victory in five minutes, at which he requests your attendance. (*Exit.*)

FLORIDA: Poor Don Faustino, my unhappy father, *ahime*, most wretched of all. (*Exit.*)

ASPASIA: If she doesn't want them, I may as well. Any fool can be uncomfortable. (*Exit.*)

Open countryside

(*Enter two SOLDIERS, one with a large gilt mirror strapped to his back, the other carrying two live chickens.*)

SOLDIER 1: Taken the war behind the enemy's lines, have you?

SOLDIER 2: Took a couple of prisoners though, didn't I?

SOLDIER 1: Drew blood myself.

SOLDIER 2: What's that thing?

SOLDIER 1: Thing?

SOLDIER 2: On your back.

SOLDIER 1: It was hanging up. It's good wood.

SOLDIER 2: You'll be hanging up on good wood if they find you with it.

SOLDIER 1: Good thing, the enemy showing the white flag like that.

SOLDIER 2: Good thing for them: we'd have cut them to ribbons.

SOLDIER 1: Good thing for us we didn't have to. Let's enjoy the truce while it lasts.

SOLDIER 2: Make a fire and cook this lot.

SOLDIER 1: Let's go.

(*Enter LISETTA carrying a basket.*)

SOLDIER 2: Let's stay.

LISETTA: Get away. Leave me be. On your way.

SOLDIER 1: You come our way. We'll show you a good time.

LISETTA: Here, mind your manners, you. I'm a good girl.

SOLDIER 2: What's in your basket?

LISETTA: Never you mind about my basket.

SOLDIER 1: You can't mean that.

SOLDIER 2: Anything you got to sell, we'll buy.

LISETTA: Well, I haven't got anything.

SOLDIER 1: You think we won't pay?

SOLDIER 2: This is money, look, now show us.

LISETTA: Cheese, eggs, fruit.

SOLDIER 2: How much the cheese?

LISETTA: Three paoli.

SOLDIER 1: And the eggs?

LISETTA: One paolo the half dozen.

SOLDIER 2: I'll give you four baiocchi for the cheese.

SOLDIER 1: Four baiocchi? What are you trying to do? Cheat the poor girl?

SOLDIER 2: What business is that of yours?

SOLDIER 1: I'm making it my business: I know you're a cheat.

SOLDIER 2: Cheat? Me? You great oaf.

SOLDIER 1: *Corponone!*

SOLDIER 2: *Birbanta!*

SOLDIER 1: *Sanguenone!*

(*They pretend to fight, finally making off with the cheese.*)

LISETTA: My eggs, my cheese, bring it back! What will my mother say? *Povera me.* (*In tears.*)

CONTE: (*Enters with CORPORAL.*) Child, child, what is the matter?

LISETTA: They stole my eggs and my cheese.

CONTE: What villains were these?

LISETTA: Two soldiers.

CONTE: Where did they go?

LISETTA: Them there, them two jumping about. Pretended to fight, and then ran off, and now they're laughing for having cheated me. Big joke for them. My mother will kill me, so she will.

CONTE: Corporal, go and arrest these two. The General gave order not a pin was to be looted during the truce, on pain of death. Take them straight to the provost-marshal and have them hanged as they deserve. And you can hang that mirror opposite them. Give them something to watch. (*CORPORAL leaves.*)

LISETTA: That's not going to get my eggs and cheese back.

CONTE: Hush, hush now. How much was it all worth?

LISETTA: Four paoli.

CONTE: All this crying for four paoli?

LISETTA: My mother will kill me, so she will.

CONTE: Come now, if it'll stop you crying, here are your four paoli.

LISETTA: Is that really four paoli?

CONTE: Do you think I'm trying to cheat you?

LISETTA: I don't trust nobody.

CONTE: I am an officer and a gentleman.

LISETTA: I'll still count them all the same.

CONTE: Well, is it all there?

LISETTA: Don't I get nothing for the fright I had?

CONTE: That is an entirely different matter. Have you nothing left to sell?

LISETTA: Fruit.

CONTE: How much?

LISETTA: Three paoli.

CONTE: Here's a zecchino.

LISETTA: I can't change your money, signore.

CONTE: Then bring it to my quarters.

LISETTA: (*In exaggerated refusal.*) *Marameo!*

CONTE: And what is that supposed to mean?

LISETTA: I'm not going to no officer's quarters.

CONTE: Your exquisite reason, child?

LISETTA: Not after what happened... to my mother.

CONTE: And what exactly did happen to your mother?

LISETTA: I don't know, but I'm not going.

CONTE: Keep your fruit then.

LISETTA: And the three paoli?

CONTE: Nothing is for nothing in this world, girl.

LISETTA: (*Crying.*) Oh, that's nice, so it is. You promise me three paoli, and now you won't give me nothing.

CONTE: (She's playing the innocent, but I think she's cunning as the devil.)

LISETTA: You said you'd give me three paoli for the fruit, what I was going to sell. Here it is then, if you don't want to pay me, who cares? (*Throws the fruit on the ground, in tears the while.*)

CONTE: I'm not refusing you three paoli, or six, or ten or whatever you want, I just want you to be nice to me.

LISETTA: I am nice.

CONTE: That's better. What's your name?

LISETTA: Lisetta.

CONTE: Is your mother alive, Lisetta?

LISETTA: Yes, and she'll kill me when...

CONTE: And your father?

LISETTA: Ehi, *poverino.* He's dead, and it's because of your war. He wore himself out chopping wood for your officers, and he just dropped dead, so you'd better give me something for my father. Who's dead.

CONTE: Come, come, whatever you want: just stop crying.

LISETTA: What'll you give me if I do?

CONTE: A scudo?

LISETTA: And if I laugh?

CONTE: A zecchino?

LISETTA: (*Laughing.*) Come on then.

CONTE: Come to my quarters.

LISETTA: Here, you can't believe none of you. Liars one and all.

CONTE: Lisetta.

LISETTA: Leave me be.

CONTE: Look at this pretty zecchino.

LISETTA: (*Laughing.*) For me?

CONTE: For you.

LISETTA: (*Laughing.*) You giving it to me?

CONTE: If you come to my quarters.

LISETTA: Rot your quarters.

CIRILLO: (*Entering, singing.*)
"*Viva la guerra, viva l'amore:*
che bel contento prova il mio cuor,
quando si trova con gioventu,
quando combatte tipetitu."
Conte, bravo, lost no time, I see.

CONTE: Don Cirillo, my dear, this young person is driving me to distraction.

CIRILLO: For why?

CONTE: She does nothing but cry or giggle. She wants money from me, and won't come to my quarters.

CIRILLO: Won't come? Won't come? And what if we were to make her come?

LISETTA: And what if you couldn't make me?

CIRILLO: You laughing at me, *fraschetta*?

LISETTA: On your way, leave me alone.

CONTE: Leave her alone, my dear: poor girl, don't make her cry.

CIRILLO: Don't you believe a word she says: I know her, a proper little devil.

LISETTA: Devils have two feet, even if one's a hoof.

CIRILLO: Now, by Heaven, that's too much.

CONTE: Come here: don't pay him any mind.

LISETTA: Where did that zecchino go to?

CONTE: Where it belongs.

LISETTA: Fine generosity. Promises me, then tricks me.

CONTE: Oh, stop crying, do.

CIRILLO: Don't believe her: dissembling slattern.

LISETTA: After all, I couldn't come to your quarters without my mother. If you was to tell her you gave me a zecchino, she might come with me.

CONTE: Oh, might she now?

CIRILLO: Damn your impudence! You hear? She'll trick you.

LISETTA: (That cripple is getting me very angry.)

CONTE: Come, I don't want to offend a pretty girl just for a zecchino.

CIRILLO: Don't give it her.

LISETTA: And what business is it of yours, you peg-legged aberration?

CONTE: Let me give it her, my dear.

CIRILLO: No, signor Conte, no.

LISETTA: Oh, devil take you. (*Runs out, kicking CIRILLO's crutch from under him.*)

CIRILLO: Help! Help me up! I'm ruined. *Oime*!

CONTE: (*Helping him up.*) Richly deserved, my dear.

CIRILLO: Did you give her the money?

CONTE: I most certainly did.

CIRILLO: You've neither brains, sense nor manners.

CONTE: You say that to me?

CIRILLO: Yes, to you. I have had skirmishes with the prettiest girls in the world and never parted with a quattrino: and you throw your money away as if the Turks were coming. *Stupido, scimunito, minchione*!

CONTE: My dear, I must ask you to moderate your tone.

CIRILLO: I've only half the legs you've got, and I could run after any woman, and beat you from a standing start, *bertuccione, vigliacco*!

CONTE: You are impertinent, sir, and over-bold.

CIRILLO: To me, sir? Impertinent? Over-bold? To me, sir?

CONTE: To you, sir, and were you not in the condition you are, I should be happy to mend your manners for you.

CIRILLO: *Corpo di bacco*, I'll fight you, sir.

CONTE: I have no mind to engage with a cripple, sir.

CIRILLO: My hands are whole, sir: we'll fight with pistols.

CONTE: Very well, sir, we'll meet at another time. (*Exit.*)

CIRILLO: Does he think to frighten me? I have fought twenty-seven duellos. I have tweaked the noses of Saracens, penetrated their seraglios, rendered their eunuchs more than naturally impotent, undone their sultanas, and would he frighten me? Ha, as I am a Christian, I am a soldier of honour, and, even limbless from the waist down, Don Cirillo will still be Don Cirillo. (*Finding a piece of paper in LISETTA's basket.*) What's here? (*Reads.*) "To the officer what undid me. This little basket and all the fruit in it is yours. Hoping you will answer the call of duty with the same industriousness as what I answered the call of love with, I remain, alas, no longer yours, Lisetta. P.S. This is not a circular." (*He hears a baby crying; looks in the basket. His worst fears are realised.*) Ah, what a fearful object is a long-neglected duty. (*Exit with the basket.*)

The quartermaster's mess

ASPASIA: Donna Florida, the armistice... Oh, I am so happy for you.

FLORIDA: *Si, cara*, for the moment, the danger to my father is past.

ASPASIA: And the danger to Don Faustino?

FLORIDA: No, I recall the arrogance with which he was prepared to be party to the death of my father. When I saw him walking towards a possible death, I felt a momentary pang, but now that he is out of danger, I remember only the cruelty with which he came to flaunt his fanatic desire for glory in my face.

ASPASIA: Officers go into battle, as they go to a party or a wedding.

FLORIDA: He might have pretended at least.

ASPASIA: Don Faustino is sincere.

FLORIDA: Your love for the military makes you their advocate. I do not, can not think as you. I loved Don Faustino before I knew his nature, and now I fear the savagery of his mind affects his very love, I fear I may find my tenderness one day harshly rewarded.

ASPASIA: Were you to see him again, maybe you would not talk like that.

FLORIDA: Maybe, but I cannot believe it.

ASPASIA: He loves you.

FLORIDA: Fine proofs of love. Has he taken the slightest pains to see me again?

ASPASIA: It might be as well to ascertain if he has come off duty yet.

FLORIDA: Oh, say rather he cares nothing for me.

ASPASIA: But you are curious to see him again, I know.

FLORIDA: Yes, I am curious to see whether he regrets not having brought home that victory which would have cost me so many tears, perhaps my life.

ASPASIA: Here he is, now you may satisfy yourself. *Addio*, Donna Florida.

FLORIDA: Where are you going?

ASPASIA: I have a pressing affair. And I should not wish your suspicions to seem prompted by me. I hope I shall find you changed soon. Oh, *cara*, love can work miracles. (*Exit.*)

FLORIDA: (*Alone.*) Perhaps, but can it persuade me to love a creature who renounces the tenderness of a loving heart for the barbarous satisfaction of a bloody victory?

FAUSTINO: (*Entering.*) Donna Florida, my prayers are answered. The truce is certain, peace is at hand: our swords will hang idle at our sides, dangers, hostilities and slaughters cease. Breathe again, *mia cara*, in the certain hope of seeing your hero father, and if you still feel any shadow of love for me, be glad to see me now, no more your enemy, but your slave, and, permit me to say it, your faithful, most fond lover. But have you still no word for me? Does not present happiness blot out all past afflictions?

FLORIDA: Don Faustino, forgive me. I do not understand.

FAUSTINO: Where is the difficulty?

FLORIDA: Was it not you who, not long since, were so happily preparing to storm the citadel, to brave my father hand to hand and face to face?

FAUSTINO: I am the same man.

FLORIDA: And now you show the same cheerfulness at an utterly contrary event? You panted to go to the battle, and can peace now be so dear to you: and can you now please to be friends with those very people for whom not an hour ago, you were desiring loss, destruction, and death?

FAUSTINO: Were I more philosopher than soldier, I could perhaps give you reasons why, in the same breast, the same happiness may be wrought by clean contrary causes. We conceive our pleasures and pains according to a state of mind moved now by affection, now by duty, sometimes by necessity, causes each one of which can take over the whole man, and it is preferable to abandon oneself to a single force than become the battlefield of conflicting passions. I was happy then in the fulfilment of my duty, as I am privileged now in the affection that binds me to you, and brings me to your feet.

FLORIDA: *Si, adorabile cavaliere*, I accept your love. Be indulgent to my foolish doubts, and set down my confusion to my shortcomings of mind and inexperience of the world.

FAUSTINO: Thank you.

FLORIDA: But when may I hope to see my father?

FAUSTINO: I cannot say precisely. The General has sent Don Ferdinando to ask his intentions. If he finds himself obliged to surrender they will propose the terms, and you should be consoled as soon as possible.

FLORIDA: Heaven send that happy moment when I may throw myself at his feet, and ask his blessing on our love.

FAUSTINO: If he were to refuse, would you for that...?

FLORIDA: I know his love for me, and...

FAUSTINO: But should an aversion conceived against me, a member of a hostile force, urge him to deny you, what would you do?

FLORIDA: I should die of grief: but duty, maybe necessity, triumphing over affection, I would study to obey my father with that same constancy with which you undertook to attack him.

FAUSTINO: Donna Florida, I must accept.

FLORIDA: Oh, now more than ever I wish to see him again.

FAUSTINO: No more earnestly than I desire the conclusion of a peace. (*Enter POLIDORO.*)

POLIDORO: Signor ensign, have you heard the news?

FAUSTINO: Is it peace?

POLIDORO: Peace, peace, pish! It is war, war, war, may it last as long as I live, and I live as long as it lasts.

FLORIDA: But what is your news?

POLIDORO: I shall deliver. Your father showed the white flag – but... he is demanding all possible military honours: unfurled standards, beating drums, covered gun carriages, arms at port, and a hundred and one other things our General will refuse to grant, and if they fail to agree, we will return to the assault, take the fort at discretion and put it to the sack.

FLORIDA: Ah, Don Faustino, and must you leave me again? Return to the fray? Expose yourself once more to the risk of cruelty towards my father?

FAUSTINO: Donna Florida, I know not what to say. You know my heart: you yourself approved my way of thinking... I pray only I shall not have to sacrifice my love to my honour.

FLORIDA: And I must once more embrace my own misfortune.

FAUSTINO: Do not seek to weaken my constancy.

POLIDORO: Signor ensign.

FAUSTINO: What the devil do you want?

POLIDORO: Your pardon: it is true Mars and Venus were good friends: but recall – Mars was caught in a net, and made a butt and a scoff.

FAUSTINO: And what might you mean by that? Think better, if you please, of an officer and a man of honour. I love a lady who deserves all love, nor shall I permit that love to be made a butt. The variance of our principles and characters dictates that for my own dignity I should spare you the treatment you so richly deserve. But if you continue to meddle in my affairs,

I shall be forced to set a term on my toleration, and put you to a well-merited correction.

POLIDORO: *Benissimo.*

FAUSTINO: Donna Florida, I must take my leave. Let me inform myself more nearly than is reported by such a dubious source. Hope in heaven, and rest assured in my love. (*Exit.*)

FLORIDA: Each moment of happiness must be paid in pain. Hopes are dupes, love agony, all confusion. (*Leaves.*)

POLIDORO: *Benissimo.* She wishes for perpetual peace, I for continual war. Thus runs the world. A farmer who wishes to sow, prays for rain; another who wishes to thresh, for sunshine. A woman who has dresses to flaunt, wishes it always fair weather; she who envies her, wishes it ever foul. Gamesters wish everyone to come to the ridotto, musicians to the ball, and actors wish them to come to the theatre, and there, thanks to you, good people, we are, for once, at one.

ACT TWO

Field of battle, with a view of the citadel of the beleaguered town, flying the white flag. The field is completely filled, a whole ox roasting on a spit, a cart with a barrel of wine, baskets of fruit and vegetables etc. A table with soldiers eating and drinking; and soldiers, peasants and women dancing. Soldiers, camp-followers engaged in buying and selling, others drawing wine from the barrel etc. A trumpet sounds and all stop to listen.

FABIO: By order of His Excellency the General Commanding, everyone is to leave the field immediately to make room for the tents to be put up.

CIRILLO: *Presto, presto,* make room there. (*To FABIO.*) Why is the General having the tents put up?

FABIO: He is to have discussions with the General of the fortress, treating for peace, and he wants to receive him here in view of the whole army.

CIRILLO: And the enemy commander is coming here in person to negotiate?

FABIO: That is what they have agreed. (*To the SOLDIERS.*) What is this, don't you obey orders any more? Move on out!

(*Exits with CIRILLO.*)

(*Drums. The SOLDIERS leave in some disorder, turning over the table, carrying everything away, knocking over the baskets. The PEASANTS cry out, the SOLDIERS beat them. Once the field is free, more SOLDIERS come and erect the General's pavilion with two seats. Trumpets and drums: SIGISMONDO comes and takes his position in his pavilion, his OFFICERS grouped around him, at the head of their troops. At a further drum signal, EGIDIO comes out of the fortress, followed by several OFFICERS, who remain in the background, while EGIDIO advances and is received by SIGISMONDO, who shows him to a seat, sitting himself on EGIDIO's left.*)

SIGISMONDO: Don Egidio, allow me to congratulate both you on a courageous defence, and your sovereign on possessing one of the most prestigious commanders of our time. Ten weeks together you have defended a citadel which should have collapsed at the very approach of our armies: I am honoured to have overcome so brave a commander. Reflect however on the condition of your fortress, the poverty of its resources, the enemy you are facing, and, if you wish us to display that humanity and condescension that brings credit to a victorious army and its commander, I must beg you to moderate somewhat of your pretensions.

EGIDIO: Don Sigismondo, your praises are no less flattering for being unmerited: a man who serves his prince does no more than his duty in serving him with loyalty. But I must tell you, you are ill-acquainted with the fortress you are besieging, that without a formal siege there is no hope of subduing it, that our provisions of food and munitions are such as will never place the garrison in any real embarrassment. I shall not speak of the courage of its defenders, of which you will have had ample proofs. We are at a point where any commander might ask for truce without dishonour. For myself, you find me ready to continue what may seem to you a reckless and superfluous defence. But I am not unaware that there might be those who would prefer an advantageous cessation of hostilities to an obstinate defence. My duty demands I maintain a just balance between daring and discretion. I therefore, according to the usages of war, displayed the white flag, demanded a truce, and here give you intention of surrender.

SIGISMONDO: I shall refuse neither the truce nor the surrender. But on what terms?

EGIDIO: On the agreed terms of warfare.

SIGISMONDO: Not all such terms are agreeable at all occasions.

EGIDIO: I cannot think my name has left me without credit.

SIGISMONDO: I shall accord more to that name than to the merit of the fort.

EGIDIO: For myself, I ask nothing. But I must demand full military honours for the standards of my sovereign.

SIGISMONDO: Come, come, Don Egidio, explain yourself: upon what terms do you intend to surrender?

EGIDIO: (*Reading from a paper.*) First that the garrison be allowed to leave the citadel under arms, with six charges allowed to every man, with standards unfurled, and drums beating. Secondly four covered gun carriages, and finally the free transport of the equipages.

SIGISMONDO: Pray forbear any further claims. The fortress is reduced to the last extremity: any such advantageous surrender is out of question. The garrison must surrender unconditionally. As a sign of respect to yourself, they will be allowed to evacuate the citadel, but with arms reversed, with furled standards and without drums. As for the gun carriages, let us not speak of them, they are not to be thought of.

EGIDIO: No. Either agree to the honours I demand, or I shall defend myself to the last drop of my blood.

SIGISMONDO: And that of how many countless others? Our army is positioned for the assault, and impatient to display its courage. You will force us to sack the city.

EGIDIO: You will not find us lacking in courage.

SIGISMONDO: Since you are so stubborn as to persist in this desperate bravado, prepare yourself for the fate of the desperate.

EGIDIO: Signore, you and I are acting in accordance with our duties. If, in the midst of this honourable dispute of arms, there is still a place for courtesy, I steel myself to ask you a favour.

SIGISMONDO: Ask. I am enemy to your arms, not to your person.

EGIDIO: Once I set foot within the beleaguered fortress, a state of war will again exist between us. Permit me, therefore, before I return to have a few brief moments with my daughter.

SIGISMONDO: The determination with which you forced me to refuse your late too great request only matches the pleasure with which I accord you this small one. Go, upon your word.

EGIDIO: Thank you. (*To his OFFICERS.*) Go back to the castle. Tell them to expect me immediately; and on pain of death, no man is to move without my orders.

SIGISMONDO: We meet again as enemies.

EGIDIO: I am impatient for that meeting.

SIGISMONDO: Beware our swords.

EGIDIO: Ours will be no less resolute.

SIGISMONDO: *Addio*, Don Egidio.

EGIDIO: *Addio*, Don Sigismondo.

(*They embrace. All leave to a fanfare. Then at the sound of drums, the stage fills up again with SOLDIERS, PEASANTS and WOMEN, dancing, eating, drinking, buying and selling as before.*)

A room in the quartermaster's mess

FLORIDA: My father in camp, and I not allowed to see him? They talk of a surrender or of a final conflict, and not a soul can tell me what is going on. I know no longer whether I more desire or dread an uncertain hope or a painful disillusion. Who's there? Who's there?

FAUSTINO: (*Enters, to FLORIDA's confusion.*) Signora, if you require a servant, here is one who will serve you till death.

FLORIDA: You here? And not a word to me? What was the outcome of the Generals' meeting? Ah no, do not tell me: in the unaccustomed sadness of your expression, I read the sadness of my own fate. My father wishes war, your General wishes war, and perhaps, beneath the feigned colours of a pretended sadness, even you applaud the massacre. Go, then, go, do not force yourself to remain. Make use of that expedient philosophy that allows you to be as happy with the love of the daughter as at the death of the father.

FAUSTINO: Calm yourself, my dearest, and your contempt: do not insult, where I do not deserve. Your tears have worn away my loyalty, and I no longer know myself. I know I love you, and I know too that a coward cannot deserve your love. But my enemy is the object of your care: I cannot be brave without appearing to you cruel.

Donna Florida, decide my fate for me. Would you have me lay my sword at my General's feet? Subscribe to my own dishonour? Expose myself to the reproaches of the camp? Suffer slights, derision, without being able to reply to my insulters? Look better at my state, and if my distress does not deserve your sympathy, let my heart at least deserve your forgiveness.

FLORIDA: Oh, God, rise, sir.

FAUSTINO: Forgive me.

FLORIDA: Rise, rise, *per carita*.

EGIDIO: (*Entering.*) *Ola*! And what are you doing at my daughter's feet?

FLORIDA: Father, oh, father!

EGIDIO: Be silent! And you, signore, explain, if you please, why you, an enemy officer, precipitate yourself at my daughter's feet with such dispatch.

FAUSTINO: Signore, to take my last farewell of her.

EGIDIO: And where do you think you are going?

FAUSTINO: To attack your city, to fight against your soldiers, and should fate present you to my sword, yourself.

EGIDIO: Your rank?

FAUSTINO: Ensign.

EGIDIO: Your pretensions to my daughter?

FAUSTINO: Those of heart and hand. The first I have from her; the second I hope to have from you.

FLORIDA: Oh, father...

EGIDIO: Be silent. I am not addressing you. Are you a gentleman?

FAUSTINO: My name is not unknown in the army.

EGIDIO: It is so far to me.

FAUSTINO: I am Don Faustino Papiri, Duke of Altomonte, Signor of Conchiglia, Cavaliere di Ripafratta, Conte di Carmagnola...

EGIDIO: I know the names. All of them.

FLORIDA: If you but knew all his qualities...

EGIDIO: Silence! You love my daughter, and have the gall to fight against her father?

FAUSTINO: A good commander knows better than I the duty of a soldier. Love does not command me before that duty.

EGIDIO: The speech of a brave man. You are worthy of my blood, whether it be to marry it or shed it.

FAUSTINO: Signore, your words encourage me to ask for your daughter's hand.

EGIDIO: You have it.

FLORIDA: When?

EGIDIO: Be silent. The situation in which we find ourselves makes it highly problematical that we shall have further speech on this subject. Do your duty, signore, assault our walls, give me proof of your courage. If you fall, death unties all knots; if I fall, and you live, avail yourself of my given word; should we both survive, the war once over, you shall have her from my hand. I hope I have said enough to a cavalier: from this moment we are enemies.

FLORIDA: Oh, *padre mio pietissimo*, do not make me die of grief.

EGIDIO: Your torments are the fruits of your own imprudence. That I consent to your marriage does not mean I approve your behaviour. A girl of noble birth, a daughter to Don Egidio, a prisoner of our enemies, does not open her heart to affections while her father sweats under arms. The good fortune to have found a noble and courageous lover is no credit to you: you might as easily have been flattered into a shameful affection.

FLORIDA: Signore, forgive me, the occasion...

EGIDIO: I do not ask for excuses, but obedience. Come with me.

FLORIDA: Where?

EGIDIO: The fortress.

FLORIDA: Would you expose me to such dangers?

EGIDIO: They will be less than those of your father and lover. Come!

FAUSTINO: Signore, have regard, to her sex, her age, her nature.

EGIDIO: All three clearly have need of better custody. If your mind is consonant with your name, you will hardly complain of my dispositions. And you – follow me without more ado.

FAUSTINO: How will you be allowed to conduct your
    daughter to the fortress?

EGIDIO: That is hardly any business of yours.

FAUSTINO: She is a prisoner of war.

EGIDIO: We are all that. I shall request permission of the
    General.

FAUSTINO: I have nothing more to say.

EGIDIO: Then it would be graceful in you to keep silent.

FLORIDA: Do you abandon me?

FAUSTINO: To your father's commands.

EGIDIO: Must I use force?

FLORIDA: Ah, no, signore. (*EGIDIO leaves.*) Don Faustino,
    my heart tells me we shall not meet again.

FAUSTINO: Hope, oh *cara*.

FLORIDA: *Addio.* I am coming, signore. (*She follows her
    father out.*)

FAUSTINO: How can I live among such afflictions? To
    scale the walls, when my heart is breaking, my foot
    stumbling, my hand trembling?

ASPASIA: (*Entering.*) Ensign, the very man.

FAUSTINO: Leave me in peace, for God's sake.

ASPASIA: I only wanted to tell you, the things you left
    with Donna Florida were looked after by me.

FAUSTINO: Not now, please.

ASPASIA: Do you not want the watch, the snuffbox, the
    rings? Do you not want them back? No? Did you say
    no? Well, I can perfectly well hold on to them. But at
    least take back your money. You will? Here then.

FAUSTINO: Oh, for Heaven's sake, leave me in peace.

ASPASIA: If you don't want it, let it lie. But what will
    Donna Florida say?

FAUSTINO: Ah, where is she now?

ASPASIA: In her quarters, I should imagine.

FAUSTINO: Did she not leave with her father?

ASPASIA: Her father?

FAUSTINO: Did you not see him?

ASPASIA: Who?

FAUSTINO: Her father.

ASPASIA: Where?

FAUSTINO: Here.

ASPASIA: Tell me, Don Faustino, is there any danger love may have turned your brain?

FAUSTINO: Where have you been all this while till now?

ASPASIA: At Orsolina's stall, buying ribbons.

FAUSTINO: Then you don't know what has happened?

ASPASIA: Not unless you tell me.

FAUSTINO: Donna Florida's father was here.

ASPASIA: Oh, Heavens!

FAUSTINO: He discovered our love.

ASPASIA: Ehi, what are you saying?

FAUSTINO: And took his daughter back to the fortress with him.

ASPASIA: Oh, what a thing now.

FAUSTINO: Are you laughing at me?

ASPASIA: No, signore, but in truth I am not weeping for you either.

FAUSTINO: Can your life so have hardened your nature?

ASPASIA: I believe I am a better soldier than you.

CONTE: (*Entering. Teasingly.*) Don Faustino, my poor fellow.

ASPASIA: You know about it too?

CONTE: I have just seen Donna Florida with her father: it was enough to make one weep.

FAUSTINO: Conte, have you come to increase my plagues?

CONTE: *Cospetto*, but you're mighty desperate in love, my dear.

ASPASIA: Cooked on both sides.

CONTE: Done to a crisp.

ASPASIA: A burnt offering to Venus.

CONTE: And where did you learn to fall in so deep? A beast that wants discourse of reason would have drawn back sooner.

FAUSTINO: Leave me alone.

ASPASIA: The ensign wishes to fight under another standard.

FAUSTINO: And you can be pleased to hold your tongue.

CONTE: Come along, my dear, a glass of canary and a good rattle of musketry will puff away the vapours of love.

FAUSTINO: I shall know my duty when the time comes.

ASPASIA: If he goes to the fight, he is afraid of offending his fair one.

FAUSTINO: Stop tormenting me.

CONTE: You will be the laughing stock of the brigade, you know.

FAUSTINO: I can bear this no longer.

ASPASIA: I'll wager they'll make lampoons on you.

FAUSTINO: Now, by God, I shall lose all patience.

ASPASIA: Beware, beware.

CIRILLO: (*Entering.*) *Animo, fratelli, corraggio.* The pioneers are at work, good moles that they are. The gunners are ready. The ladders are prepared. The army is massing and we await only the signal for the attack.

ASPASIA: Softly, softly, Don Cirillo, or this poor ensign will succumb.

CIRILLO: Ehi, I saw your friend.

FAUSTINO: I must beg you to keep your nose out of my affairs: or I shall demand satisfaction.

CIRILLO: Whenever you please. Pistols and no quarter. Come one, come all. I have not forgotten you either, Conte.

CONTE: Whenever you please, my dear. But for the present we must make a pact of no aggression to comfort this poor passionate beast.

FAUSTINO: Would you drive me past endurance?

CIRILLO: But what the devil do you think the army will say of you? In love? Forsooth, *buon viaggio*! Are there no other women in the world?
(*Sings.*) "We all shall lead much happier lives
By getting rid of tedious wives
Who only scold by night and day
Over the hills and far away."

FAUSTINO: Now you are impertinent, sir.
(*Trumpet.*)

CONTE: To the breach, my dears. (*Exit.*)

CIRILLO: Victory. (*Exit.*)

FAUSTINO: Or death. (*Exit.*)

ASPASIA: Come back safe.

POLIDORO: (*Entering.*) What is going on?

ASPASIA: The truce was soon over. The citadel refused to surrender, and it is agreed they shall take it by storm.

POLIDORO: Then the war is not over yet? *Benissimo.*

ASPASIA: However, when this campaign is done, I shall not be withdrawing to winter quarters.

POLIDORO: What are you saying, daughter? Do you seek to ruin me? It is only in winter quarters that money has the mastery over morality. Even soldiers eat less in summer. But, with January and February as enemies, they are more eager to draw at a bottle than a sword. Added to which, the officers find themselves in a sudden most desperate need for fur coats, and I have made sufficient provision of them to cover a regiment, and make a clean profit of fifty thousand zecchini.

ASPASIA: Am I to lead this kind of life for ever? Am I never to hear music in four-four time and not feel I have to march to it?

POLIDORO: And what else did you have in mind, girl?

ASPASIA: Marriage.

POLIDORO: *Benissimo.* And using what for a husband?

ASPASIA: An officer.

POLIDORO: And be widowed in three days?

ASPASIA: *Benissimo.*

POLIDORO: *Figlia mia*, I do not advise you to take an officer.

ASPASIA: And why not, pray?

POLIDORO: Officers are for the most part younger sons: they have little money of their own, and what they have they have a tendency to squander. And they are as free with their lives. Yesterday at the assault I saw a young fellow at the head of his platoon, carrying nothing but one of those little sticks, rattan, I sell them for a couple of zecchini, and a good line they are too. The first shell landed wide: he wagged his little stick at the enemy gunners and said: "Butterfingers!" – and the next volley took his head off. But if they are careless of their lives (and a widow unprovided for is a melancholy creature) they are all too nice on points of honour. For fear of an unfashionable jealousy, they let their wives be courted by one and all, but for the merest nothing you will see them, a sword in one hand, cudgel in 'tother, the sword to run through monsieur, the cudgel to compliment madame.

ASPASIA: Well, in this case, madame will know well enough how to reply to the importuning of monsieur whoever. I am used to the army, and will not permit myself to be overruled. You understand me?

POLIDORO: *Benissimo.*

ASPASIA: *Signor padre,* I want to get married, *benissimo*? It is your business to provide me with a dowry, *benissimo*? And if ever, by accident or design or misfortune you should have the tenderness to thwart me in this, I have protectors in the regiment who will know how to change your mind for you, *prestissimo, benissimo*? *Serva, signor padre.* (*Exit.*)

POLIDORO: Oh, one can't say the army hasn't made a man of her. I deserve worse. And here is my dear Orsolina, now there is a true woman for you: charm, worth, prudence, thrift and industry, and every inch of it for me.

ORSOLINA: (*Entering in some distress.*) *Ahi, ahi, signor commissario.*

POLIDORO: Orsolina, you here? Who's minding the stall? What the devil?

ORSOLINA: The devil exactly. I've been running.

POLIDORO: What has happened?

ORSOLINA: After they published the truce, I opened up two tables of faro: hoping to make more profit, I put everything I had into them: four officers came in to play, and in twenty minutes broke the bank at both tables, and here you see me without a farthing.

POLIDORO: And my money?

ORSOLINA: Gone to the devil with all the rest.

POLIDORO: Then you can go after it to fetch it back.

ORSOLINA: Softly, now. This time may have gone badly. Next time we can still clean them out. Remember what you promised me?

POLIDORO: Let me tell you, clearly, roundly and precisely, our acquaintance ceased several seconds ago.

ORSOLINA: Then let me tell you clearly, roundly and precisely, that if you do not maintain your promise to me, I shall find myself compelled to seek out the General, and reveal somewhat of your monopolies to him: money on usury at twenty and thirty per cent; flour adulterated with chickpeas, rye and chaff; you have interests in the gambling, the wine-shops and the lotteries; instead of going to the forests for wood, to save on the wagons, you devastate the countryside, tearing up trees, vines, and the props that hold them up, while you prop up every good-for-nothing in the army. *Sissignore*, and if that is not enough, I have another little secret or two which I shall be delighted to regale you with at your earliest convenience. *La riverisco, divotamente.* (*She goes out.*)

POLIDORO: A fulsome eulogy, but by no means inept. The threat is opportune. She is well capable of carrying it into effect. She is a woman. She had a need. I made her a promise. I made her a confidant. She could ruin me. There is only one way I can keep her mouth shut. *Benissimo.* (*He follows her out.*)

Open sparsely-wooded country

FERDINANDO: I have been done the most notorious wrong, I tell you.

CORPORAL: How would that be, signore?

FERDINANDO: Everyone else is ordered to the assault, and why do they order me to look after this dismal jakes of a place? Do they think I am not brave enough? Don Faustino was promoted after I was: why should he be given the honour of taking part in, nay leading part of the assault, and I this unenviable station?

CORPORAL: For my part I'm glad to be here. Less chance of getting picked off.

FERDINANDO: Pooh, you talk like an enlisted man.

CORPORAL: I am an enlisted man.

FERDINANDO: Where the danger is greatest, so is the honour.

CORPORAL: Death would be different for officers, then?

FERDINANDO: Don Faustino should not have been preferred over my head.

CORPORAL: The General must have thought highly of you to have put you here.

FERDINANDO: I'm not complaining about the General.

CORPORAL: Oh, who, then?

FERDINANDO: That wretched Don Faustino, trying to get the vantage of me, wheedling his way into the front ranks.

CORPORAL: I shouldn't think so this time: he's in love with Donna Florida, and she's back in the fortress with her father. I expect he's looking forward to taking them both prisoner. Or worse.

FERDINANDO: Is that true?

CORPORAL: Would I make it up?

FERDINANDO: Then perhaps her tears will damp his ardour. (*Trumpet.*) Where is that coming from?

CORPORAL: Over there.

FERDINANDO: Who is it?

CORPORAL: Man on horseback. At the gallop.

FERDINANDO: Corporal, challenge that man.

CORPORAL: Right away, signore. Who goes there?

COURIER: (*Entering on horseback, at the gallop.*) Friend. A despatch for the General.

CORPORAL: You hear, signore?

FERDINANDO: Give him two soldiers as escort.

CORPORAL: You there, escort this man to the General's headquarters.

FERDINANDO: What's the news out there?

COURIER: Peace. (*Falls in a dead faint.*)

FERDINANDO: You mean they've signed?

CORPORAL: Seems so.

FERDINANDO: Quickly, two men, take horses, and get this man to the General quick as you can.

CORPORAL: All the rest stand fast. You two, along of him. Dismiss.

FERDINANDO: And watch your neck.

COURIER: I've fallen twice already. I haven't got a breath left in me. (*The COURIER leaves with two SOLDIERS.*)

CORPORAL: Good news, then, signore?

FERDINANDO: Good news that Don Faustino will not now have the chance to crow over me with all his deeds of heroism at the assault. No, that at least he cannot do. (*Goes out.*)

CORPORAL: Envy never enters an empty house, they say, but it sticks like pitch to soldiers, and what have they got when all's done? The only profession that can be congratulated on reaching old age. (*Goes out after FERDINANDO.*)

The Battlefield

(*The battlefield with batteries of cannon. The white flag is no longer flying from the fortress. FAUSTINO, the CONTE, FABIO. SOLDIERS, led by the CONTE, move in to scale the walls. SOLDIERS in the fortress, defending themselves. Drums. A fanfare breaks into the sound of the drums, which fall silent. Voices are heard over the field, shouting:* "Peace! Peace!" *The assailants retire from the walls, retreat into camp, and form up in order. SIGISMONDO enters with a paper.*)

SIGISMONDO: *Amici*, the despatch from His Majesty. The sovereigns have concluded a peace: it is published. It remains for me to praise your courage, to make mention of it to your sovereign, and ensure that you reap a just reward for these and other desserts. Three cheers for His Majesty. Hip, hip... Don Fabio, you will make it your care to see that the wounded are brought off, and to bury the dead. Don Faustino, if your wounds will permit, I give you the honour of presenting the peace terms to the honourable commander who inflicted them. And bring Don Ferdinando to me, immediately.
(*SIGISMONDO gives a paper to FAUSTINO, who runs enthusiastically towards the citadel. At a signal with his*

handkerchief, the bridge is lowered over the moat, the trumpets sound inside the fortress, and he enters.)

CIRILLO: *Evviva la pace*!

POLIDORO: Lieutenant, what is going on? Has peace broken out?

CIRILLO: Ask the General.

POLIDORO: Eccellenza, forgive me, but is it peace?

SIGISMONDO: That is so, commissario, here is the despatch.

POLIDORO: *Benissimo.*

SIGISMONDO: I have, by the same packet, a further despatch that concerns you alone.

POLIDORO: *Benissimo.*

SIGISMONDO: An order from the High Command to remove you forthwith from the post of quartermaster. You are to render up complete accounts of your stewardship, and you will remain under open arrest until they are approved by the Auditor-General.

CIRILLO: *Benissimo, signor commissario*?

ORSOLINA: Well, *signor commissario*, do you remember what you said to me?

POLIDORO: I told you to go to the devil, and I'm now telling you to get back to him.

ORSOLINA: Then I shall have to speak to the General. Eccellenza, the fact is, Don Polidoro...

SIGISMONDO: Don Polidoro has been dismissed the service, and you, being party to his malpractices, will accompany him from the camp.

ORSOLINA: Ahi, *pazienza*. Don Polidoro, do you hear? I shall have to go back to laundering.

POLIDORO: And I to driving mules.

ASPASIA: (*Entering in haste.*) Ah, Eccellenza, I have heard of the misfortune that has befallen my father. I cannot say whether his disgrace be merited or no, I know only that I am left a wretched creature, and my fate is uncertain to say the very least.

SIGISMONDO: Marry, child: marry whom you will. I shall see your dowry is provided for out of your father's ample depredations.

POLIDORO: But, Eccellenza...

SIGISMONDO: Be silent.

POLIDORO: *Benissimo.* I am mum. (*Goes.*)

ASPASIA: Your Excellency's charity does him honour. May
Heaven soon present me with a match.

CIRILLO: (*Presenting himself.*) It has already.

ASPASIA: Thank you. You may be able to fill a breach:
I prefer a husband who can fill a pair of breeches.

FERDINANDO: (*Entering with the CORPORAL.*) *Eccomi,*
Eccellenza, at your orders.

SIGISMONDO: Don Ferdinando, I understand you complain
of me.

FERDINANDO: I, signore?

SIGISMONDO: You, signore. The duty to which you
were assigned was sufficiently honourable: you chose to
see it otherwise, through the mist of an ambition to
which I set down your imprudence. In future respect
better the orders of those in authority, and make a
virtue of obedience. And you may begin by making the
acquaintance of a commander who may have greater
sway over you than I. (*Indicates ASPASIA.*)

FERDINANDO: Your Excellency is most kind. But forgive
me, how did you get wind of my resentment?

SIGISMONDO: The only secrets safe in camp are the
enemy's. I have no lack of informants.

CORPORAL: How else does one live on a corporal's pay?
(*Fanfare from the citadel. Enter EGIDIO, FLORIDA, FAUSTINO,
with SOLDIERS etc. Answering fanfare from the camp, then drums.*)

EGIDIO: Signore, I am pleased to meet you again, and in
friendship.

SIGISMONDO: A friendship ever dear to me.

EGIDIO: (*Presenting FLORIDA.*) My daughter.

SIGISMONDO: I congratulate her on her father.

EGIDIO: And, if your authority permits, on her bridegroom.

FAUSTINO: Signore, the heart that braved the perils of
Mars was not proof against the onslaughts of Cupid, and
if I have triumphed in war, I hope not to be reproved if
I now surrender to love.

SIGISMONDO: An honest love does not dishonour a hero.
You have my authority.

FAUSTINO: I am obliged to your Excellency.

FLORIDA: I too thank the General. I ask my father's pardon for having disposed of my heart without him, and in their presences, I take my husband's hand.

CIRILLO: *Viva l'amore, viva la pace!*

FAUSTINO: Don Cirillo, are we friends or enemies?

CIRILLO: Friends, friends, with all the world.

CONTE: (*Carried in on a shutter, badly wounded.*) And with me?

CIRILLO: Conte, with you, though when you are recovered, we may have a bout for old times' sake, and I fancy on more equal terms.

CONTE: My dear, I am delighted. (*To FAUSTINO.*) Will you permit me to be of your party at winter quarters?

FAUSTINO: Of my party, but not of my wife's.

CONTE: You must beware, you really must, my dear. (*Dies.*)

FLORIDA: Have you not glory enough?

SIGISMONDO: Gentlemen, and lovers, to your respective quarters. Prayers will be offered for peace in ten minutes. I expect your attendance. (*Everyone leaves, FLORIDA giving a last look at the CONTE's body.*)

FLORIDA: And so the wars are done.

(*She leaves too. CIRILLO comes forward to address the audience.*)

CIRILLO: *Signori, signore miei benignissimi*, who have so patiently witnessed this presentation of *La Guerra*, I have an apology. The author of this comedy forgot one little thing. He forgot to mention which countries were actually doing the fighting, and the name of the place they were fighting over. We actors might have remedied this slight omission, but respect for our text held us back, for once. This only I will say, that all the nations of the world go to war in the same way, and all of them are strong, courageous, intrepid and glorious, if only in the eyes of those who fight for them; and to all of them we wish peace. And to you, most humane of audiences, whom, we are sure, are among those few who have the wisdom, prudence and moderation to desire peace, we wish it too.